"Jeff Kemp's *Facing the Blitz* is a game-changer for every man. What you'll find in these pages is that Kemp is the Life Coach you need to successfully execute with purpose and resolve. Suit up and read this book—it's game time!"

—Dr. Dennis Rainey
President and CEO, FamilyLife

"Former NFL quarterback Jeff Kemp knows well that blitzes can knock you flat on your back—but if you're prepared, you can beat the blitz for a huge play. In *Facing the Blitz*, Kemp transforms this on-field knowledge into real-life wisdom, teaching you how to beat the blitzes in your life and turn them into victories."

—William Bennett, former U.S. Secretary of Education
and host of the nationally syndicated
talk show *Morning in America*

"If you like football, you'll love this book. But Jeff Kemp's sage advice applies to much more than the gridiron. Every one of us will be confronted by seemingly insurmountable odds at some point. *Facing the Blitz* provides solid, biblical advice for confronting life's most difficult challenges."

—Jim Daly, president, Focus on the Family

"Dads face problems, and so do their kids. *Facing the Blitz* gives us riveting stories and strategies to live well and help our children overcome and thrive."

—Mark Merrill, president, Family First;
author, *All Pro Dad: Seven Essentials
to Be a Hero to Your Kids*

"This book could change your life—or help you to help another who has suffered a 'blitz'—a devastating loss, defeat, or humiliation. Jeff Kemp, a former pro quarterback and a faith-filled family advocate, inspires us by citing examples in his own life and others', to understand that we can convert a terrible present into a bright future."

—Mort Kondracke, political journalist

"As a quarterback in college and professional ranks, Jeff Kemp knows the blitz well and gives us preparation and training for life's blitzes. He is a very transparent guy and, as you read this book, you will want to share it with others. This is a message not only for men but for women as well."

—Darrel Billups, ThD, executive director,
National Coalition of Ministries to Men

"When I first read the title of Jeff's book *Facing the Blitz*, it put a smile on my face. As a former quarterback and then a quarterback coach, it was my job to prepare athletes for the possibility of overwhelming attack. Jeff Kemp was a great quarterback and a wonderful student. He was as prepared as any quarterback I have coached to handle the blitz as well as other difficult situations on the field. Now he has taken the lessons he learned on the field and applied them to life. This book is a must-read for all of us. Tests and trials are a part of the human condition; no one is immune to the challenges of facing adversity. My hope is that, by reading this book, we all may be better equipped to deal with tough situations and emerge stronger and wiser from the experience."

—Mike Holmgren, former head coach,
Super Bowl Champion Green Bay Packers

"Jeff is a man of deep faith, love, and leadership. I have tremendous admiration for Jeff and his approach to living a complete and healthy life. He's as prepared to face the blitz as well as anyone I know—and I'm not talking about just when he was an NFL quarterback. Read, learn, and apply. Valuable lessons for life's greatest challenges."

—Jim Nantz, CBS sportscaster

"*Facing the Blitz* is a gem full of wisdom and hope and practical advice for anyone who fears suffering and difficulty. It's easy to read, remember, and use. Amazing!"

—Pat Lencioni, president, The Table Group;
bestselling author of *The Advantage*
and *The Five Dysfunctions of a Team*

FACING THE BLITZ

THREE STRATEGIES
FOR TURNING TRIALS
INTO TRIUMPHS

JEFF KEMP

BETHANYHOUSEPUBLISHERS

a division of Baker Publishing Group
Minneapolis, Minnesota

© 2015 by Jeff Kemp

Published by Bethany House Publishers
11400 Hampshire Avenue South
Bloomington, Minnesota 55438
www.bethanyhouse.com

Bethany House Publishers is a division of
Baker Publishing Group, Grand Rapids, Michigan

Printed in the United States of America

Library of Congress Cataloging-in-Publication Data
Kemp, Jeff.
    Facing the blitz : three strategies for turning trials into triumphs / Jeff Kemp ; foreword by Tony Dungy.
        pages cm
    Includes bibliographical references.
    Summary: "Popular speaker and former NFL quarterback Jeff Kemp shows how challenges in life are like blitzes in football—both are opportunities one can turn to an advantage"—Provided by publisher.
    ISBN 978-0-7642-1402-8 (cloth : alk. paper)
    1. Conduct of life. 2. Success. I. Title.
BJ1589.K456 2015
158—dc23   2014043578

Cover design by Dan Pitts

Author is represented by Alive Communications, Inc.

15   16   17   18   19   20   21   7   6   5   4   3   2   1

I dedicate this message to my universally loved mom, Joanne Kemp, who has always modeled the faith, hope, and love that fueled our family and allowed my dad to be the champion father he was. I also dedicate it to my greatest teammate and love, Stacy . . . and to our family, Kyle and Lindsay Ann, Kory and Dana, Kolby and Keegan. Who you are and how you lift others excites me!

Contents

Contents

Acknowledgments

To be very clear, quarterbacks—and husbands—can't do anything without help; we depend deeply on others. If we forget that or take it for granted, we are fooling ourselves and dishonoring our team. A lineman can make great blocks on his own. A defender can tackle on his own. But a quarterback can't complete a pass without a whole lot of help from his teammates. He can't even start the play until the ball is snapped to him. And as for how much a wife helps a husband (and especially how much Stacy helps me), that's a bigger job than a quarterback's!

In that spirit, I have a lot of people to thank for help on this book. Beating blitzes and turning life's troubles into triumphs is essentially about teamwork, and I have been blessed with amazing teammates, advisors, and friends. My best friend and ultimate teammate, who has faced the most blitzes with me, is my wife. Stacy, thank you for your unconditional love, your dedicated faith in the Lord, your courageous truth-telling, your prayers, your wisdom, and your perspective. What I'm especially grateful for is your heroic dedication and excellence in shaping our family and our home. You are my benchmark for being a love investor. We've laughed about how "helpable" I am, but I celebrate that I married the world's strongest helper. Your beauty is inside and out, and your legacy will be magnificent.

I'd like to thank my friend and mentor Don Wallis for his encouragement on my fiftieth birthday to trust my life experiences and lessons, and to feel comfortable sharing them. I would pass the same encouragement on to others who hit the halfway mark (give or take a few years). Don, your self-revealing humility and mentoring will always shape me.

A few years ago I lost my closest buddy and a man who helped me grow to know Jesus and His ways. I am so grateful for Chuck Obremski, our Rams chaplain who taught Scripture, loved well, and used his cancer blitz to bless countless people. Chuck finished strong!

So much of what I've learned and so many of my laughs come from our sons. Kyle, Kory, Kolby, and Keegan, thank you for being so honest, real, and funny. You've given me the greatest of laughs and joy; thanks for letting me share our stories. Special thanks to my sister Jennifer for her early encouragement and improvements to this book. And to my mom, Joanne; sister, Judith; and brother, Jimmy, for their joyful roles in my life. Mom, you are inspirational to all of us. The message of this book emanates from your faith and practicing the "power of the personal." This book is a thanks to you and Dad, as so many of the gifts you gave us birthed the ideas and principles that fill my heart and these pages.

I'd like to thank my friend Gary Thomas, who helped me embark on this journey. The heavy lifting was done with an awesome teammate and editor, Arlyn Lawrence. Arlyn, thank you for your prayers, talent, dedication, sympathetic spirit, and huge contribution to this mission. May your family and all your writing be blessed so that others may be encouraged. Thanks to Joel, Brian, Lisa, and Rick at Alive Communications, and to Andy, Amanda, Carra, and Shaun at Bethany House. Pat Lencioni, Jeremy Vallerand, Bryan Coley, Dr. Shawn Stoever, Dennis Trittin, Dr. Dave Mashburn—you men rolled up your sleeves to help me in many ways. I am very grateful. Dr. Scott Sticksel, you out-blessed me again, and your leadership coaching shaped me and the ideas in this book greatly. Bill Bennett, your friendship to Dad and our family inspired the acronym *LIFT* to describe my dad. Thank you. Thanks to Phil Hotsenpiller of New York Executive Coaching. Rick Schirmer, Dr. Jeff Fray, Dr. Gary Oliver, and Dr. John Trent—you have inspired my passion and vision. Thanks to talented encouragers Sealy Yates, Gary Smalley, Wes Yoder, Jerry Brewer, Jeff Abramovitz, Tim Popadic, David Huckabee, Peb Jackson, Mark Merrill, and Les Parrott. Special thanks to our team leader at FamilyLife, Dennis Rainey, and to Bob Lepine, Leslie Barner, Jim Whitmore, and Pete McIndoe, among many who fuel my passion for lifting men and marriages.

I have special thanks for my gutsy, generous, and noble friend Dave Ederer. Your story, example, and invitation to Jan and Ken's Wild Adventure are central to beating blitzes and living lives that lift others to their best. And thank you, Jan Janura, Ken Tada, Chris Leech, and all my other "Welcome to Manhood" buddies who've adventured to share their stories and inspire my sons and each other. I'd like to thank my post–football huddle friends Tom Flick, Mike Clark, and Jim Zorn—you guys are a team for life. Jon Sharpe, Bob Nuber, Jerry Brown, Fred, Dean, Tom, and Barry of my C-3 Thursday morning group—thanks for walking with me through a great blitz, as did my awesome Friday Seattle guys led by Matt McIlwain. Thank you, Jason Pederson and Big Ray Roberts. Ray, you're a treasured friend and a masterpiece in the making.

The lives and stories of so many weave the tapestry of my life and this book. I'm grateful to Coach Bill Walsh and Coach Mike Holmgren for one intense season of my career and many lessons for life. Coaches John Robinson, Chuck Knox, and Mike Swider, along with Norm Evans, George Toles, Eugene Robinson, Reggie White, Keith Jackson, Brent Jones, Jerry Rice, Paul Skansi, Steve Dils, George Lilja, Jackie Slater, Pat Haden, George Andrews, and a couple hundred other teammates are in my mind as I pen these acknowledgments. Thank you, men. I'm grateful for the greatest sport in history—football—and the NFL. I'm glad Dad taught me—and I loved teaching my four sons—the lessons that epitomize the best of sport.

Leslie Mayne, Jerry Brown, Steve and Tricia Woodworth, Steve and Terry Largent, Clark and Joan Donnell, Marvin and Jeanette Charles, Coach Tony Dungy—to all of you who have faced life's intense blitzes and allowed them to mold and spur you to bless other people, including me, thank you so much. I'm grateful to offer small glimpses into the pain and beauty of your stories. Noel Meador, General Jimmy Collins, and board members and supporters of Stronger Families have been huge blessings in my life and proof of the silver linings that come from tough times.

My gratitude and acknowledgments are inadequate. Ultimately, I'm aware that I really can do nothing of lasting value or virtue apart from my total dependence on my heavenly Father and Lord Jesus Christ. I hope people show grace to me for any errors or self-infected words in this book, and that any credit accrues to God, who alone is perfect in truth and love.

Foreword

Most football fans today are familiar with the term *blitz*—a strategy where the defensive team attempts to disrupt their opponent with a quick, devastating, and hopefully unexpected attack. During my football career I had the unique experience of being on both sides of the blitz. As a defensive back for the Pittsburgh Steelers, I was part of a unit that executed blitzes well enough to win a Super Bowl championship in 1979. But before that, I had been a college quarterback and for four years had been on the receiving end of those blitzes. I learned that no matter how much you prepared for them, it was still possible to get hit by a blitz you didn't see coming. The key, then, was how you would respond after getting thrown for a loss.

Those lessons I learned as a quarterback on how to deal with blitzes helped me become not only a better football player but a better person as well, because life can deal you unexpected setbacks that can hit you harder than any blitzing linebacker. Although I feel I've been extremely blessed by God, I've still had to deal with some things I never saw coming. Getting injured, getting traded as a player, and getting fired as a coach were not pleasant times. Losing my parents to diabetes and leukemia hit me even harder. But I had learned that how you move forward from those things is the key.

In 2005, though, my family and I faced what for us was the ultimate blitz. Our eighteen-year-old son, James, took his own life. He was a wonderful young man, very sensitive and caring. We've never experienced any greater pain. Such a loss can put a tremendous strain on a marriage. It can push you away from loved ones—or it can pull you together. You can push away from God or draw close to a compassionate heavenly Father. We drew together as a family, and we committed ourselves to drawing closer to God. Since then, we have continued to call upon His power, a power so much greater than our own, to face life's trials.

The entire momentum of an NFL game can turn as the result of a blitz. Surprise attacks, brutal blows, and intense trials are the essence of the game, and life is no different. We will have unexpected challenges, painful losses, and intense difficulties—the loss of a loved one, a surprise medical diagnosis, the loss of a job . . . And just like the quarterback, our job in life is not to merely survive the blitz, it's to beat it.

If we want to succeed in life, we need to know how to face the blitz, how to overcome our trials, and how to turn what seems bad into good . . . for ourselves and others. The truth is, although there are great dangers in the blitz, there are also great opportunities. Opportunities to respond, adapt, and succeed. Some of football's greatest touchdowns have come under the duress of the blitz.

My friend Jeff Kemp tells a compelling story of facing life's blitzes. Jeff was a long-shot to quarterback in the NFL for eleven seasons, but he comes from a family where leadership, teamwork, and perseverance are ways of life. Compassion for the oppressed and beleaguered was a mark of his father, Jack, himself a legendary NFL quarterback and widely admired American statesman. Continuing in that legacy, Jeff has devoted his post-football life to strengthening marriages and families to increase their care and love for their children.

In *Facing the Blitz*, Jeff shares time-tested strategies for overcoming blitzes at home, at the office, and in key relationships. Jeff delivers a practical game plan, drawn from his experience on the field and in the grip of challenges off the field.

You'll learn how champions in the NFL—and those who overcome in life—have done it through mutually uplifting relationships, through sacrifice, and by allowing Jesus Christ to be their guide when the going gets tough. They have enough humility to put the team, the cause, and others before themselves. Those who persevere together find that the blitzes and challenges become a joy and a blessing to others.

The stories and truths in this book will inspire, encourage, and equip you to face real life. You will discover how your pain can result in transcendent gain. Your mess can become a message, a hope-giving testimony pointing to a *greater* hope and love.

This book will make a difference in your life. You'll want to read, digest, and re-read it. I hope you share it with friends to help them through their own difficulties and to strengthen their important teams, from family to business to sports.

—Tony Dungy, author of *Uncommon: Finding Your Path to Significance*

Introduction

Life isn't always as we dreamed it should be and wanted it to be. It's wonderful but hard. It's tragic but poignant. It's beautiful but flawed. It goes along pretty well, and then things can fall apart and blow up really badly. But that is not always the direction things go, from good to bad. Things also go from bad to good, from painful trial to positive building block, from suffering to healing, from needing comfort to comforting others, and from feeling overwhelmed to overcoming.

I know my biggest losses and toughest times have yielded value in their own way, often more so than the easier and triumphant moments. I've learned about joys that don't fade when our circumstances tank. I've traveled pathways that carried me from lost to found. I've seen the destructive consequences of self-first, self-only living be turned around by the transformative power of humility and unconditional love. That's why I know we all have the capacity to overcome our blitzes.

The problem is, we are all so incredibly imperfect.

I grew up around football teams during my father's career in professional football and as a player myself. In my eleven-season wild ride as an NFL quarterback, I played on many fine teams for many dedicated coaches and several truly exceptional ones. I also grew up with an epic encourager in my dad, Jack Kemp. He was an amazing man who, after his thirteen seasons of pro football, turned to a life of public service in the intense and volatile world of political leadership. He embodied and instilled in me an energizing approach to life: LIFT—Life Is For Transformation. He was the one who first and most importantly taught me how to beat life's blitzes and transform them into opportunities to *lift* others around me.

I've been on this faith-deepening journey for over thirty years. Since ending my football career, I've invested myself in a career to strengthen the priorities, commitments, and skills needed to build healthy families. Because of these experiences, I've come to see life through the lens of teams, leadership, and relationships.

Most of what I have learned in my journey has come with the help of other people and their friendship, perspective, and coaching. My passion is that these stories and lessons enrich your journey and help you successfully face your own blitzes in life.

Think back to a huge hurt or loss in your life, such as an injustice, disappointment, or humiliation. Maybe you lost a job, were betrayed by someone you loved, or publicly failed at something important to you. Did it blindside you? Did it take you down so hard that you thought you might not recover? Did it feel like a physical punch in the gut?

If your response to any of the above is yes, then you, friend, have been on the receiving end of a BLITZ.

The word *blitz* has been a part of my vocabulary throughout my life. When I was a boy, I played youth football and watched my dad play professionally in the NFL. Later, when I too played in the NFL, I learned firsthand the horror and the beauty of the blitz, both literally and figuratively, for eleven seasons.

I wouldn't have guessed that my experience handling blitzes on and off the field would provide me with many of the most powerful lessons of my life. And I certainly didn't expect it to make the difference between a life of meaning and one of despair. But that's been my reality—and probably yours too. Isn't life, for all of us, about facing blitzes?

The purpose of this book is to share the lessons I learned (and keep learning) from dealing with blitzes, so that you can avoid unnecessary fear, setback, and misery when circumstances fall short of what you want them to be, and instead experience courage, growth, gratitude, and joy.

If you'll take a long-term perspective, if you're willing to change, and if you adopt an others-centered approach to everyday living, then life's problems, attacks, and trials will serve to *grow* you. They will grow your humility, your honesty, your relationships, your faith, and your joy. They will open up your eyes to the pain that others are feeling because of their blitzes and help you be a better team player and support person for them. These are all good things that can come out of your blitzes.

You'll learn that overcoming is not about bouncing back so much as bouncing UP. No matter how near or how far you are from your blitz, this is not a book about the past. It's about the present and future. This is a message about recovering, about coming back from, about transforming—and then getting better and going further than you ever dreamed possible.

But to do all that, you'll need the courage to embrace three simple principles—*strategies*, if you will—which are as easy to understand as they are difficult to follow:

1. Take a long-term view.
2. Be willing to change.
3. Reach out to others.

Before you dive into understanding and trying to employ the three strategies for facing, and beating, a blitz, you'll need to understand why some people are better at it than others, and why for other people these requirements don't make any sense. It all has to do with how we see ourselves, the world, and life in general. How well you master these strategies will depend on how you answer these questions:

1. Do you see life as an individual sport or a team sport?
2. Do you look at the world from the standpoint of a consumer or an investor?
3. What is your power source for living, loving, and overcoming trials?

Your answers to these questions will reveal your lenses. You'll know what I mean if you've ever had your eyes examined. During the exam, you rest your chin in a vision device while the optometrist swaps out multiple lenses until you can see clearly. You need the right lenses in order to see properly. By the same token, once we can see well, we're better equipped to face life's blitzes. Keep considering these questions as you read through this book.

What are your life lenses today, and what do you want them to be?

Take a Long-Term View

> Find the Opportunity in the Crisis
> Let the Old Dream Die
> Embrace a Bigger Vision

1

Find the Opportunity in the Crisis

blitz: *noun* \blits\
   a: *blitzkrieg*, an intensive all-out aerial attack or campaign
   b: a sudden overwhelming bombardment
   c: a rush of the passer by a defensive linebacker, back, or end
   in football[1]

As a former NFL quarterback, I've seen more than my share of blitzes, including one in a crucial late-season game against the Houston Oilers when I was playing for the Philadelphia Eagles. It was *Monday Night Football*, and facing each other that night were two teams with the toughest defenses in the NFL. Despite talented players on both offenses, it would be a game remembered for big hits and all-out blitzes.

For those who don't know the game well, a blitz is what happens when an excessive number of defensive players approach the line of scrimmage with the intention of rushing the quarterback and sacking him for a significant loss in yards. The goals are surprise and intimidation, meant to overwhelm and damage an offense's play, as well as the quarterback!

23

Derived from the term *blitzkrieg* used in World War II, it's the idea of throwing sudden and extra resources at an enemy in order to bring about shock, panic, and defeat. But when the enemy adapts to a blitz and refuses to panic, it can be a great opportunity for success. Here's a look into what it was like that Monday night in the NFL.

We were in the Houston Astrodome, aka the "House of Pain," the term that was adopted as a tribute to the jackhammer defense that made it incredibly difficult for any visiting team to escape without loss or injury. Well into the third quarter, the Oilers' defense was dominating and stymieing our offense. Thanks to our phenomenal defense, who brought their own version of pain that night, we were tied 3–3.

Our first-string quarterback, Jim McMahon, had been hammered and injured. Tough as he was, he had to leave the game, and I came in. Other than three plays, followed by a concussion and a trip to the hospital a few weeks earlier, this was my first chance to quarterback the Eagles.

It was my first drive of the game, and we had worked our way to the Oilers' twenty-yard line, where it was third and eight. The coach called for a deep, slow-developing drop-back pass to our tight end, Keith Jackson. As we broke the huddle and I approached the line of scrimmage, I knew I would need good protection from my offensive line. The rabid defense of the Oilers made that unlikely. The linebackers' gleaming eyes and their tightened alignment told me they had no intention of dropping back to cover our receivers; these guys were coming after *me*, the new backup quarterback. It was a blitz.

As I called out my signals, the linebackers and linemen excitedly called out their own signals, no doubt trying to confuse me and drown out the sound of my voice. They howled, "Gap!" "Slide!" "Randy!" "Switch!" The crowd was wild, the situation crucial, and the adrenaline began pumping as I stood behind the center whose right hand gripped the football.

The instant the ball hit my hands, pandemonium broke loose. Houston threw everything they had in my direction. Two extra linebackers were bearing down on me, with the free safety approaching at a sprint after having snuck up to the line of scrimmage. It was a full blitz, an all-out attack.

Keep in mind, I was playing for my life that night in Houston. I was nearing the end of my career, and my future with the team hung in the balance. The NFL isn't exactly a secure workplace due to the intense competition of earning your job back every week, sudden injuries, and career obsolescence by age thirty. As I dropped back, I was fully aware that in the next few seconds something very bad—or very good—was about to happen.

The Good, the Bad, and the Opportunity

We are all faced with a series of great opportunities brilliantly disguised as impossible situation.

Charles Swindoll

Since retiring from football more than two decades ago, I've become more and more aware of life's blitzes *outside* the stadium. A child is born with a disability; a loved one is injured or diagnosed with a terminal disease; the bank calls in your company loan and you can't cover it; the boss tells you you've been laid off. Or you lose your savings in the stock market, your best friend to a cross-country move, or your spouse to an affair or divorce.

Blitzes like this happen every day. And the way we face them makes all the difference in the world. It can bring something very good out of something very bad.

Many of us, when facing a life blitz, only see the negative and not the opportunity. Others fail to see the bigger picture in the blitz until they're looking back at it in hindsight. Then there are those people who come alive during blitzes. They learn, change, and adapt, realizing blitzes are trials that can force change and open up new opportunities we could never have imagined before.

Trials can humble and even hurt us, but they can also teach and motivate us. It all depends on the attitude we bring to the blitz.

The key is our *lens*: If we get bogged down by the frustration of the circumstances and think only about survival, a blitz will be primarily negative and possibly devastating. However, if our mind-set is to look for something more, for the blessing hidden amidst the challenge, a blitz gives us a chance to live our lives at an entirely different level.

> Far better it is to dare mighty things, to win glorious triumphs, even though checkered by failure, than to take rank with those poor spirits who neither enjoy much nor suffer much, because they live in the gray twilight that knows not victory nor defeat.
>
> Theodore Roosevelt

At its core, a life blitz—the unexpected problem, the deep trial, the shocking loss—contains the power to bring out the best inside each of us. It can open us up to growth and experiences and positives that wouldn't have otherwise occurred. It shakes us free from our old routines and paradigms in a way nothing else can. We might not ever *choose* a blitz—few people do—but we can aim to *use* it when one comes our way.

The way I came to play for the Philadelphia Eagles before that memorable and adrenaline-pumping night at the Astrodome was the result of a personal blitz of my own. I had begun my eleventh and what was to be my last season of professional football in a precarious position as the fourth-string quarterback for the Seattle Seahawks. I began that year behind the previous season's starter, Dave Krieg, and two younger QBs who'd been first-round draft picks. Things didn't look good for me there. But by the second regular season game, I had not only made the team, I'd become the starter.

During the time I was quarterbacking, the Seahawks won three games and lost three, the last defeat being an overtime loss against the Los Angeles Raiders. Unfortunately, my errant pass to Raider safety Ronnie Lott cost us the game—and me my job. I was cut two days later, mid-season. To go from being the starting quarterback of a team to an unemployed one facing retirement, all in just a few days' time, is about as difficult as life gets in the NFL. It was definitely a blitz.

That night, after being cut, my then-six-year-old son, Kyle, said the prayer at our dinner table. He thanked God for the food, then prayed for me. "God, please give Daddy a new team. And I want it to be the Eagles."

Kyle wasn't an astute follower of professional football. He was only six. In fact, he had no clue that Philadelphia even had an NFL team named the Eagles. His first-grade youth soccer team was named the Eagles, so he was just hoping I'd play for a team with the same name as his!

It was a pivotal day in my life. I'd been booed, benched, and traded before, but this felt heavier. Yet my wife, Stacy, and I had learned to trust God through all those prior trials and the intense ups and downs of pro football. I knew that I shouldn't focus on the negative possibilities of my circumstances. Even if it had been the end of my career, I didn't need to let that plunge me into anger or depression—it would only create bigger problems for me and my family. It was no time to panic or despair, as tempting as that can be for any of us in the heat of the blitz.

Amazingly, the next morning I got a call from the Philadelphia Eagles, wanting to sign me up to play for the rest of the season. On the other end of the phone I heard, "Jeff, Randall Cunningham is out with a broken leg, Jim McMahon's battling injuries, and we need an experienced QB who's ready to play." A few weeks later, I was on the field in the Astrodome in that critical game against the Oilers, where I was hit hard by a blitz of an entirely different dimension.

Back to the Astrodome

Thankfully, during my time in the league, I had learned not to panic at the sight of a full-on blitz. In fact, the first thought that went through my head that night was, *If I move quickly enough, we've got a touchdown.*

Since I'm only six feet tall and the wall of linemen coming at me each averaged about six-foot-five, I couldn't see downfield very well. What did become clear to me was the sprinting free safety who slipped through the line untouched and leaped at me with a sadistic scowl on his face. Actually, I have no idea about the look on his face. I was busy trying to find my tight end. I couldn't see much with so many Houston players blitzing, especially with the free safety in my face. It was an eclipse . . . and time was running out!

But my mind was racing in a good way. Because the free safety had left his regular defensive zone, it meant the deep middle was uncovered. I had to take a shot downfield. It was a risk because, if I got sacked, even a field goal was uncertain. Still, the opportunity was there, and I wasn't the only one who saw it.

Seeing the blitz attack triggered adaptations by others on our offense. Our All-Pro tight end, Keith Jackson, abandoned his late-developing corner route and ran a quick post route to the uncovered middle. The ball flew from my hand and hurtled past the ear hole of the blitzing free safety, who had his hands up in an attempt to further block my vision. I couldn't see where Keith was, so I threw the ball to where I thought he should be, being careful to give it just enough arc to get it over the defender and for Keith to get under it for the catch.

As the ball left my hand, I felt the full impact of the charging free safety's weight. He collided with my chest and landed directly on top of me. Some defensive players like to take their time getting off the quarterback, maybe even letting a few choice words and spit escape from their mouths while they're piled on top of you. I don't remember worrying about any of that. While the free safety had me knocked down, he hadn't ended the play. We'd gotten the pass off.

Unable to see what was happening, I listened to the crowd. I knew if there was an immediate roar in our opponent's domed stadium, it would signal that I'd just thrown an interception. If there was a quick cheer followed by applause, I'd know the ball had fallen incomplete.

But there was none of that. Instead, it was deathly silent . . . a sweet sound. In a visiting stadium, silence is great news.

Keith had played it perfectly. Changing his route to a quick post, the ball met him just over the shoulder. Not only did he catch it, he crossed the goal line for what would be the game's only—and winning—touchdown. The Philadelphia Eagles won the game 13–6 in the House of Pain. We hadn't merely survived the blitz; we'd turned it into an opportunity greater than anything we could have created on our own.

Finding the Opportunity in Your Crisis

That blitz by the Oilers could have taken the Eagles right out of the game. As it turned out, though, our best play of the game came on what could have been the worst. It all depended on whether we would let the blitz beat us or choose to respond to the opportunity hidden within it.

What does it take to break a blitz and turn it to your advantage?

Danger   Opportunity

The Chinese character for *crisis* combines two smaller characters: one representing danger, and one representing opportunity. That's the intrinsic nature of a crisis. You may be asking, "Can my something bad really turn into good?" I believe so, and nearly every day I meet other people who think so too—and who prove it.

I think of the server I met in a restaurant in Gig Harbor, Washington. Leslie was a middle-aged mom who told me the story of her adult son's tragic death. He was a soldier who had served in Iraq. When he returned home, he suffered from PTSD. He died away from her, but here in the states, not in the war. The pain of losing a child, Leslie told me, is like no other. She'll never forget the day she picked up the phone and heard the voice of Kyle's father telling her the news, "We've lost our boy."

Her friends helped her up when she fell to the floor, that day and many more after it. They flew her to Virginia, where she went through the motions of burial and the recovery of Kyle's meager belongings. Her friends encouraged her, prayed for her, and refused to let her drown alone in her tears. But there was one thing they could not do for her. They could not beat her blitz for her. She had to do that herself. Or, as Leslie would put it, she had to beat it with God's help.

At first she had tried to numb the pain with medication and alcohol, but that gave little relief. That's when she turned to God. She'd had experience with what she called "lip-service Christianity," but now God became a reality in her life. Praying He would bring her some sort of purpose and peace in the midst of her turmoil, she began to look for Him in everything she could—in the people, the places, and even the little things she encountered every day, both the good and the bad.

Then, providentially, a friend who didn't know about Kyle's death called her and invited her to New Orleans to help chaperone a youth group traveling there to serve people devastated by Hurricane Katrina. The trip changed her perspective—and her life. She'd been the sufferer, and now she was serving others who were suffering. A spark of life, and healing, ignited in her.

"I know God didn't cause Kyle's death," Leslie regularly tells people. "I still have lots to praise Him for, no matter how bad things get. You can't blame God for the bad if you want to praise Him for the good at the same time.

"I can show my three other kids, who are still here, that you can get through something like this. You can miss Kyle, but you can still go forward and turn this into an opportunity to serve other soldiers. You've got to be patient in the process and learn the lessons in the losses."

Serving other soldiers is precisely the way that Leslie has used her blitz for opportunity and found healing and hope. The restaurant where she works teamed up with her to host a free luncheon for over ninety Green Berets headed to Afghanistan. She organizes the Race for a Soldier, a community-wide half marathon to raise awareness and support for suffering soldiers returning to civilian life. She's out to save lives and families. Her mission has given her the healing, purpose, and joy that had nearly been extinguished by a blitz. Leslie's lesson in the loss? "Take your bad, serve somebody else, and turn it to good."[2]

Sometimes, as Leslie experienced, a blitz turns into something amazing you can give away to others. Other times the blitz brings new direction and empowerment to you personally. Just ask epic Olympic swimmer Michael Phelps.

Everyone knows that training is the key to success in Olympic swimming. But just ten months before the 2008 Olympics, Michael Phelps tripped in a parking lot and fractured his wrist. Skeptics forecasted the worst, and hopes for Olympic glory dimmed. Phelps, however, figured out a new path. Unable to continue his normal training, he decided to train with his legs, develop his kick, and stay in the pool with his teammates, using a kickboard to support his wrist.

Ultimately, the injury to Phelps's wrist proved to be more of a catalyst than a crisis. He used it to develop the astounding and exceptional kick that helped him blow away the competition, come from behind, and win eight Olympic gold medals.

Crisis or catalyst? Hang in there, friend; be creative and persevere. Bad things can still turn out for good. You wouldn't be the first person who, after a blitz, woke up to the realization that you'd lost focus on the simpler things of life. Blitzes can direct us back to the fundamentals, the essentials of life.

It's not always easy or appropriate to tell someone there are riches to be mined when they're in the midst of pain, in the trial of a lifetime, or engulfed in the heartache of losing a loved one. But it is appropriate, truthful, and compassionate to encourage people with the reality that new life can spring from death, a bright future can follow a terrible present, and that a better you can emerge from the greatest difficulty you've ever faced.

I know this, because the toughest things I've gone through personally have given me the best lessons and platform to be able to encourage others. I've been disappointed, overlooked, rejected, traded, cut, booed by sixty thousand fans, and injured. I left football much earlier than I wanted to. I've lost big games and blown great opportunities to become a long-term starting NFL QB. I've watched money disappear in investments, the stock market, and in big contracts that never cashed because I was released from the team.

When I was leading a nonprofit organization, budget crunches forced me to release highly valued people at crucial junctures. When the economic slump created an intense funding crisis, the only option for salvaging our organization was for me to resign, extract my salary, and let go numerous devoted people, triggering blitzes in their personal lives and family finances.

And the most personally devastating: My family lost my father to terminal cancer—a swift five-month departure of my greatest encourager, and a legacy-shaping man in our family and our nation.

Some of your blitzes may make mine sound tame in comparison, but the principle applies in every case: The same blitz that threatens to destroy you can also build you. The lens through which you view the blitz—and the way you use it—will make the difference between whether you travel the path of relational support and personal growth or fall helplessly into the chasm of despair and bitterness. Certainly, when viewed from our limited vantage point, life seems unfair. Yet allowing oneself to be a victim takes away our hope and the power to overcome.

If you're in the midst of a blitz right now, or recovering from one, the decisions you make in the coming months will shape you for years to come. We can't always choose what happens to us, but we can always choose our response. That, in turn, will shape what kind of person we become. It will also shape the degree to which we become an encourager and helper in the lives of others. The blitz is not the *end* of the story; it's only the catalyst to a greater one.

Time Out for Self-Reflection

1. What "life blitz" are you experiencing right now or have you experienced recently?

2. What are the potential (or actual) losses you're facing?

3. What are the potential *opportunities*? Think long term, positively, and try to come up with at least one, if not more, such as an area of personal growth, an important lesson, or openness to a new opportunity.

Run the Play: Practical Application

1. Start looking for and writing down examples of blitzes that have been turned around for good—in your life, in others' lives, in history, sports, politics, medicine, the arts and sciences.

2. Find a person you respect for his or her resilience and character, and ask how they've faced their blitzes. Look for principles and record what you learn.

My prayer for you:

Perfect Creator, Loving Father, Lord Jesus,

Please be present and real to the unique person reading this. Open the eyes of their heart and bring wisdom to their mind. Comfort them and strengthen them through their blitz and the response to past blitzes. Give them faith to be grateful and positive in turning to you when facing troubles, trials, and losses. Help them convert what seems bad into something good that can grow faith and character, improve relationships, and lift others. Bring your hope, your love, your power, and your Spirit to them as they read this book and live its message.

2

Let the Old Dream Die

Endings are a natural part of growth. Determine whether a "season" has passed. . . . The sooner you put an end to things that stall your growth, the better.

Dr. Henry Cloud, author of *Necessary Endings*

Blitzes have many faces. Steve Largent, a teammate and friend, has faced blitzes on the field as well as any player in football. His unsurpassed competitiveness and football intelligence have earned him membership in the NFL Hall of Fame. Steve and his wife, Terry, have also faced blitzes in their family. One happened suddenly with the birth of their fourth child. Steve tells about it in his own words:

> We were elated over our new little boy. Then the doctor turned him over on his stomach, and I saw the problem—our son, Kramer, had been born with spina bifida, a defect that left part of his spinal cord exposed. I felt like my world had come crashing down. I thought of all the things Kramer would never be able to do as a normal, healthy child.

I'm convinced, now, that there's only one way I was able to handle my initial pain and disappointment—and that's with God's help. I want Kramer to grow up and know that his mom and dad could joyfully accept his birth, because we realize God created him, accepts him, and loves him just as he is.

That perspective, that lens, is what enabled us to overcome our blitz, and what will help Kramer to overcome his.

Steve and Terry didn't handle their blitz alone. One of the ways God's help showed up in their lives was through another couple, Clark and Joan Donnell, who had recently faced the same blitz with their daughter. The Donnells and Largents became friends. Compassion and coaching became real through each others' experiences, as they faced similar challenges.

Teamwork is crucial to facing a blitz. In the Donnells' experience, Steve and Terry were able to see a couple who had the dream of perfect health dashed for their daughter, yet who refocused on the new reality of loving and embracing the uniquely valuable person she is. Many things were made more difficult. Certain dreams were gone. But two wonderful babies with medical challenges grew up in loving families and have since become awesome young adults. Additionally, both families developed a heightened compassion for and new role as encouragers to other families. "I'm a way more empathetic and patient person now," says Steve, "largely in part to what we've gone through with Kramer."

Letting the Old Dream Go

An important truth about blitzes is that they destroy the original play. A new play or adaptation replaces the old one. Great things can happen, but they will happen in a different way. The dream you had in your head as you walked out of the huddle and up to the line of scrimmage needs to be held lightly. That doesn't mean you don't have faith or confidence in running that play. You can still move the team and the ball down the field. But you can't be so rigid or locked in to an expectation or dream of how things will go that it makes you inflexible in what you think you'll do on the play.

Most quarterbacks will remember that some of our dumbest throws were intercepted because we "predetermined" where we would throw and which receiver would receive the ball. Our mind and emotions told us, *He'll be open. It'll be a big play.* But in reality it turned out different, and we weren't careful to read the situation and adjust. We threw it anyway, into the teeth of the defense we didn't expect—and the result was not good.

When a blitz comes, the offense had better be able to quickly let the past play die, put it aside, and make the needed adjustments. Other times, an offense will sense a blitz before the ball is snapped. The quarterback may have time to call an audible or give a hand signal to a receiver to change a route. The old play is cancelled and a new one is called. But even if you loved the last play, the circumstances have changed.

You've got to be willing to let the old play go. The blitz may mean it's time to come up with a new one. And fast.

Walking Out of Your Blitz

No matter what form your blitz has taken, it's up to you to get up and face it before you can overcome it and walk out of it. Here's what you can do:

1. Acknowledge your blitz for what it is. FACE REALITY.

Sometimes a blitz happens to us and we don't call it what it is so it can be faced. It may be an immediate circumstance, in which case it'll be fairly obvious, such as a family or marriage crisis, a financial collapse, a career loss, a health issue, or the loss of a loved one.

Your blitz may be subtle, deeper, and more long-standing than an immediate crisis. It may be an abusive childhood, the divorce of your parents, the taunting of childhood playmates that left you with scars, or missed opportunities for education or career from which you have never really recovered. In such cases, you may have never recognized that what you were going through was indeed a blitz. If you didn't cause it, don't blame yourself.

2. Resist the urge to point the finger at those you think are responsible. SELF-REFLECT.

In some blitzes you may have played a role in what happened to you, or how you responded to it. Embrace the humility to slow down and face the blitz through self-reflection. Ask yourself, *What part did I play in this crisis, failure, or problem,* as small as it may be, *and what can I do about it?* Maybe an honest look inside convinces you that you're only 10 percent responsible, but owning even that small percentage is the most empowering thing you can do. If you say you had no role in it, that the blame rests totally on others, you've just labeled yourself a victim. You've neutralized yourself. You've given away your ability to effect change and improve things.

In most cases, there will be things you can learn—not only by looking at the cause of the event, but at your response to it. *Did I make things worse? Could I have been better prepared? What was revealed about my priorities? Did I isolate? Did I lash out? Did I choose not to forgive and instead nurture my bitterness?*

A caveat here: If you were abused, hurt, or neglected as a child, or abused by someone who exploited your weaknesses with their power, I'm not referring to your situation. You're not at fault. You may benefit from professional counseling and/or the spiritual guidance of a pastor, priest, or rabbi. You didn't cause or deserve that abuse. But your blitz may still be turned for the good of protecting and healing others.

3. Approach others with humility. HUMBLE YOURSELF.

Humility recognizes that we are flawed and that others are flawed. It helps us to face and learn from reality without throwing fuel on the fire by punishing others or ourselves. A lot of us—guys, especially—tend to look down on humble people. We sometimes think humility is a sign of weakness. Many athletes, military, and business people, both men and women, fear the thought of ever appearing weak, so they go out of their way not to look humble. But humility is a strength. It improves relationships and can heal conflict.

What kind of office do you want to work in? What kind of home do you want to live in? What kind of team do you want to play on? One where everyone pulls for themselves, or one where everyone looks out for the others? Where people are pulling each other down or lifting each other up?

Humility attracts; pride repels. Pride may turn you into a celebrity, but it'll never lead to intimacy. Even if you do succeed by climbing over everyone else, you won't enjoy it very much; you won't have anyone to enjoy it with, and it's not likely to last very long.

The Role of Forgiveness

Forgiveness is a gift you give yourself.

Michele Weiner-Davis

Sometimes a dream is not the only thing that needs to die. Sometimes it's a grudge. How important is forgiveness in beating a blitz? I can't say it strongly enough: It's *crucial.*

Martin Luther once said, "I cannot help it if a bird lands on my head. I can help it if the bird builds a nest there." Basically, unforgiveness is like letting a bird build a nest in your head. It's choosing to hold on to a grudge, offense, or sense of injustice. It's holding on to blame and bitterness toward someone. What we don't realize is that it always weighs *us* down.

A woman rides in a wheelchair bearing the sign: *Hit by a drunk driver in 1987.* She's living her life defined by her accident, cemented to her blitz. That's what bitterness does. It defines us by our offenses and injustices. It traps and damages us far more than the people toward whom we direct it. It locks us into an identity forever tied to our (perceived) victimization—unless we are willing to forgive.

I see this freedom of forgiveness in the lives of my friends Steve and Tricia Woodworth, who lost their seventeen-year-old son, Joel, to a car accident in 2011. Joel had been a difficult child to raise. Adopted along with his twin sister, he had battled with fetal alcohol syndrome, anger outbursts, drug abuse, and other issues, particularly from the onset of puberty.

Shortly before his death, Joel had willingly undergone a year of residential treatment at a highly structured program for troubled teens. He returned home a sober, hopeful man: cooperative, relational, and deeply interested in God. Soon, though, Joel started to slip again. Two days after he got his driver's license, he attended a party where teens were drinking alcohol. Joel wasn't drinking; he was the designated driver. However, when that party broke up, Joel drove to his friend's house, where he did begin to drink. There are different stories about what exactly happened next, but in the end, Joel found himself in the passenger's seat next to his best friend, who didn't even have a driver's license and had also been drinking.

Only a mile from home, Joel's friend lost control and slammed the car into a utility pole, killing both himself and Joel instantly, with the car erupting into flames. The next morning there was a knock on the Woodworths' door. Steve answered it, and every parent's nightmare began to unfold. Standing on the porch were two women from the coroner's office and a chaplain.

The very next day, Tricia—in the midst of her own grief—went directly to the other boy's house. She had loved Joel's friend—he had been calling her "Mom" for years—and since she considered herself a second mom to him, this was like losing two of her children. Yet she looked past her own grief, dropped everything, and went to check on and comfort the other boy's mother.

"We were not mad at God. Not for one minute were we mad at God," Tricia says. "Nor were we mad at her. She was like a deer in the headlights. I knocked at the door; she opened it. She grabbed me and simply said, 'Our babies . . .'"

The two women bonded like sisters. They began spending time together. As they grieved together, it was only natural for Tricia to share the source of her peace with her struggling new friend. She shared with the woman that her source for healing was her relationship with Jesus Christ and the hope she had from trusting in God. Attorneys advised the Woodworths to sue, but for the Woodworths, this wasn't an option.

"Would it bring the boys back?" Tricia asks rhetorically. "Of course not. The best thing to do is to forgive and move on." Now Tricia considers the woman one of her closest friends.

Both Steve and Tricia point out the principle in this story: **You have to let go of the right to be angry and get redress.** They both asked, "How can God be glorified from the deaths of these precious boys?" They realized they would suffer more if they took legal action; they would all be dragged through the mud. Instead, they looked for the positives—every single one they could possibly find to help them overcome their blitz and help others around them.

Be Patient

You can't look for justice for your blitz in short-time horizons. Football blitzes can *sometimes* convert to success instantaneously. It's what makes football so fun to watch and is a good metaphor for overcoming hard blows. But even in football, a blitz that sacks the quarterback early in the game may not be converted to success by the offense until late in the game. It doesn't come until *after* they have re-huddled on the sideline or in the locker room at half time, and *after* they've made the needed adjustments and preparations for how to handle a similar blitz.

And *that* blitz may not come until the fourth quarter. The defense attacks the offense, committing the safeties to attack rather than defend. The coverage is man-to-man and vulnerable to a deep pass or breakaway catch and run. Finally, the offense seizes the opportunity and throws a touchdown to win the game. Hold that illustration in tension with the fact that life's time cycles are much longer than the seven seconds of a football play or three hours of a game. That's strategy number one. *We've got to learn to take the long view.*

It's long-term thinking that helps us not only get up from and recover from our blitz, but enables us to look ahead to the next play. We can come up with a new play. We can embrace a new and greater vision. And that's what the next chapter is all about.

Time Out for Self-Reflection

1. Is there a dream you're holding on to that no longer matches reality and is holding you back?

2. What steps have you taken to face and walk out of your blitz? Are you willing to (a) face reality, (b) self-reflect, and (c) humble yourself?

3. With those steps in mind, is there anyone you need to forgive, anything you need to let go? To paraphrase Martin Luther, "Is there a bird's nest you need to get out of your hair?" If so, who or what? What's your action step?

4. Is there a person you should speak with, or at least write, to begin a healing? Ask them for forgiveness, grant them forgiveness, put the past away.

Run the Play: Practical Application

1. Write down a dream you need to let go of on a piece of paper. Rip it up, crumple it, or burn it.

2. Write down what you want to learn and how you want to grow beyond this blitz.

3. Write down the names of any persons or groups you need to forgive. Decide to cancel any bitterness toward them and any negative judgments about them. Set yourself free from negative thoughts that trap you in past pain or disappointment.

3

Embrace a Bigger Vision

Vision is the art of seeing what is invisible to others.

Jonathan Swift

I've played twenty seasons of football in my life, and I was the predicted starter during preseason in only one of all those years. But it was never my *goal* to be a second-stringer.

I may have been a third-string quarterback my junior year in high school, sat on the bench for two years at Dartmouth, and slipped into the NFL as a surprise undrafted free agent, but I did not aspire to get into the league only to become a backup. I had a vision. My dream was to become a starting quarterback and take my team to the Super Bowl. Really no quarterback in the league would be worth his salt if he dreamed and believed anything less, would he?

I thought I had my chance when in 1987 the Seattle Seahawks acquired me in a trade from the San Francisco 49ers to compete with starting quarterback Dave Krieg. They thought I could either push Dave to be better while providing the team with an excellent backup, or beat him out and become the starter myself.

In that first year, the season was shortened by a strike, so I didn't have the time I needed to surpass him. But early in the following season, Dave was injured, and I had my opportunity to play. This was my chance to step up, my time to get the focused attention of the coaches, to improve every week, to win games, and ultimately, help aim our team toward the Super Bowl and achieve my dream.

Why expect anything else? I'd always been a late-blooming underdog who had consistently risen to the challenge, exceeded expectations, and helped my teams to win games. The movement was always upward, despite occasional setbacks. We'd gone to the playoffs in 1984 when I first quarterbacked for the Rams. I'd done really well for the 49ers in 1986 while playing for the injured Joe Montana, the team's legendary star. But then I injured my hip, and Joe made a miraculous return from back surgery to masterful performances. After the season, the team determined to bring in the highly talented and touted Steve Young to be Montana's backup and future replacement. I was swiftly thanked and traded to Seattle. It was a blow, but not a knockout.

That was how I ended up back on the bench in Seattle, backing up Dave Krieg. That is, until Dave fell injured in San Diego and I was suddenly slated to start the following week against my old team, the 49ers: Bill Walsh, Mike Holmgren, Joe Montana, Ronnie Lott, and crew. My thought: *Finally, I'm getting my real shot at this. The perseverance and the dreaming are about to be realized. This is my chance with the Seahawks. I'm finally getting the opportunity to accomplish my dream.*

It was an excellent week of intense practice with lots of extra time in film study. Then there was the carb-heavy pregame team meal Sunday morning at a local hotel, out of which I emerged feeling positive—and I wasn't the only one. A key offensive coach walked up to me as we exited the dining room, and he put his arm around me and said, "Jeff, I've been waiting for the day that you would be the Seahawks' quarterback. . . . You're going to do great." It was a rare degree of personal encouragement for the NFL, where coaches tend to motivate more by pressure, intimidation, and threat. This, on the other hand, felt great. I felt affirmed, valued, connected, and confident.

The elation was short-lived. On the first series of plays in the game, we ran twice and hardly advanced the ball. It was third down with eight to go to keep the drive alive. I threw a pass to Steve Largent, who ran a slant route and split two defenders. I put the ball right into his hands, and . . . he dropped it.

Remember, this was Steve Largent, the best player on our team and one of the greatest receivers in history, with hands so good that if he touched the ball, you could pretty well count on him catching it. For Steve to drop a ball was almost unheard of.

Realistically, a quarterback needs to have thick skin and let things roll off his shoulders like water off a duck's back. You can't let the disappointment of a sack, incompletion, interception, or some other mistake occupy your thoughts for more than a fraction of a second. Quickly move on to the next opportunity. The most important moment is not the one that just happened; it's the one that's about to happen.

So at that point I wasn't fazed by it, although I admit I joked to myself, *Come on, Steve. What's up? You're dropping a ball on me in my first game! You're my buddy, my closest friend! You're Mr. Dependable. I've never seen you drop a pass. Now you do it against the Niners? In a big opportunity against the team that traded me to Seattle?*

That's part of football: tough bounces, mistakes. I let it roll off my back. It was just one play. Steve dropped a pass. But after that, it wasn't Steve who made mistakes, it was I.

I started to play poorly, worse than I'd ever played before, even going back to youth football. I could barely complete a pass or get a first down. I was playing *horribly*. Our whole team was playing badly, and, in contrast, the 49ers were playing lights-out. At the half we were losing 28–0 and I'd only completed four passes, and three of those were to the wrong team! I was being booed by a stadium full of Seahawk fans. I'd never experienced this before, which didn't matter to me as much as the fact that we were losing so disastrously, at a very crucial time for both our team and for me personally.

At half time, I was fully ready to tap in to the positive, overcome-the-odds, persevere-and-never-give-in attitude my father had instilled in me. Always fight for a comeback. At the same time, I was halfway intelligent enough to understand the reality that I was playing abysmally and we were in big trouble. This was professional football, where players are paid to win, and the coaches would probably bench me. Yet I desperately wanted the chance to stay in the game. I wanted to play the way I knew I could to turn the game around and fight for a victory, long as the odds may be.

Of my three first-half interceptions, one was a Hail Mary desperation pass at the end of the half. Getting that frantic last-second-of-the-half pass intercepted wasn't so bad, but the other two interceptions were big deals, costly mistakes. I realized after the interceptions that the 49ers were jamming our tight end at the line of scrimmage. They were effectively preventing him from getting down the middle of the field to stretch the two safeties and create the option that someone would be open when we ran corner routes by the outside receivers. I got an idea to put the tight end in motion so that he would avoid the jam and release successfully down the middle of the field.

I walked up to the offensive coach, the one who'd been so encouraging to me at the hotel before the game, hoping to share this idea I thought would help us in the second half. However, as I approached him, it was clear that his previous goodwill toward me had dissipated. Not only was he NOT interested in my ideas, he wasn't interested in keeping me in the game either. I was three feet from him when I began with, "Coach . . ."

He turned his back on me, ignored me, and called another quarterback to be put into the game instead. He didn't even acknowledge me, not for the whole second half. The head coach confirmed that I wouldn't be going back in. I was being benched.

The feelings of failure and rejection and lost opportunity were brutally intense. It felt like my gut was dropping out of me as I saw my chance slipping away in only one half of a single game. They hadn't seen me at anywhere near my normal self, much less my best self.

Worse yet, I wasn't only being judged and rejected from a *performance* standpoint, but it was carrying over into a *relationship* standpoint in an extreme way. I stood by the coach and encouraged the other quarterback for the rest of the game, but I never heard another word from that previously encouraging coach. He had thoroughly lost his excitement about me as the Seahawks' quarterback.

I have to insert here that he isn't a bad guy. He wasn't trying to punish me. He simply was not finding value in me anymore. My performance had let him and the team down. And as a result of his value system, there was no more relational connection from him toward me. He didn't chat with me anymore or acknowledge me in the hallway or locker room. I had failed. I had not lived up to his expectations or his encouragement. He stopped talking to me in meetings with the offensive players and didn't inquire about my opinions on plays we would run or defenses we would watch on video to prepare for games. For the next month, whenever I saw him in the hallway, his eyes would veer away from me to avoid contact. The relationship had been completely closed off.

I don't tell this story to demonize him. In other arenas he's a good guy and a good coach. But he was living in the pressure cooker of pro football, which perhaps is only slightly more pressured and cutthroat than society at large. This coach, who had dropped any relationship with me when my performance failed, was a victim himself, affected by a value system he was passing right on down to me. Head coaches, team owners—those people above him—were operating in the same value system. Conditional. Performance-based.

And that's the point.

Getting a Bigger Perspective

What I've just described is the dominant value system of the society in which we live—a conditional, performance-based, what-have-you-done-for-me-lately value system. It's all over our society.

Wall Street measures companies and people in dollars and determines value by short-term quarterly earnings estimates or daily stock prices. Madison Avenue's advertising machines push it, making us addicts to having the newest and most impressive products in order to feel adequate, whole, and happy. You've felt it—at work, in school, and in social circles.

Happiness is presented conditionally, largely shaped by our performance-related success and enjoyment of whatever is being sold to us. Hollywood's assessment of television and movie actors' worth and popularity is notoriously fickle, leaving many stars to wonder if anyone really values them as people or wants a real relationship. They're haunted by the fear that they are only valued for the benefits of their celebrity status. The irony of deep insecurity in famous people is played out in the dumb and desperate things they often do.

Business employees in a down economy or a downsizing company also know this value system. So do professional athletes. In fact, I think I can safely say that anyone who says they have not seen or felt it must have skipped junior high school!

One week I was the rising new quarterback, generating optimistic expectations and super-affirming encouragement from a key coach. Thirty minutes of football later, I was a failure. Ignored by that coach. Benched. Dreams were dashed pretty darn quickly. Rejection stings.

If you've ever experienced this particular kind of blitz, you know exactly what I mean.

Losing my briefest chance to be the Seahawks starter hurt. I was relegated to third string. It was the most painful and gut-wrenching season of my life. But I wasn't alone. I faced it with Stacy, a few close friends on the team, and a quickly deepening relationship with and dependence on God. That's the team that helped me handle my rejection and embrace a bigger vision. I grew, yet not before I ached. My poor thirty minutes of football caused me to be viewed totally differently by coaches, players, and the media, particularly following my demotion to third string.

I remember soaking in the pain of my failure and demotion one evening after practice. I'd come home to our apartment and Stacy had put our two young sons to bed. I was lying on my back on the floor and started to release my pent-up feelings to her. I had such big goals and had always been confident. I'd also handled setbacks in the past with the strong undergirding of my relationship and faith in God. This one was harder, deeper, more painful. Hope for my career was invisible. I felt the sniffles and sobs of tears pressing in on me.

What hurt the most at that point was not just to fail and be demoted so drastically, but knowing how much it really affected me, especially when I'd expected my faith to be more mature. It was depressing to realize how much I'd let my situation impact me, when I'd been aiming to count on God more than my circumstances. That was a low point, but it was also a window that allowed me to see a crucial paradigm and contrast in life.

After that blitz with the Seahawks, I gained a bigger perspective, a different lens. I could clearly see the *conditional, performance-based value system* that dominates our lives. I could see its faulty nature and that there was a better way to view and value people and relationships. I've grown to embrace a deeper reality and more hopeful value system on which to base my life: *an unconditional, relationally based value system*. In essence it is a value system of love—real love.

Real love—and I'm not referring to the romantic kind here—isn't just a feeling of liking something or being attracted to someone. Real love for people is a decision, a choice. It shapes our feelings but doesn't depend on them. It chooses to value and add value to another person simply because of his or her intrinsic worth as a human being. It desires the best and does what is best for another person, even when that person is neither lovable nor demonstrating merit to be loved. It's not conditional; it's relational. It's not about taking, but giving. It's not about consuming from others for our benefit, but investing in them for their benefit. Finding and adopting this value system is essential for overcoming every blitz you will ever face.

Find a New Value System

That's why your team at home is so important—we need our families. Blitzes are a time to prioritize relationships, face issues, and build something more intimate and real than we ever had before. That's what my friend Steve Woodworth experienced in dealing with the grief, loss, and injustice surrounding his son's death.

Steve admits he tried to keep Joel from returning to his childhood friend. The program Joel went through emphasized the importance of staying away from old friends with whom you had formed bad habits. But Steve knew he had to let go of his anger. He had to learn to accept God's sovereignty and that God was in control. And he had to learn to lean on others, which was hard for both him and Tricia.

Steve says now, "With all the bad things that happened in our life with Joel, I came to believe that God sees the end from the beginning. There were good years and bad years. I think I would be a real jerk if all these trials hadn't taught me, humbled me, and softened me. Knowing that helped me in dealing with Joel's death. I knew that God was going to do something good for us in this, no matter how awful it was.

"Everyone who had heard about Joel's death and had also lost a child reached out, like my friend Jerry. At first I felt like I should man up and go back to work, but Jerry said, 'Don't do it!' Then he informed me that whenever I did go back, I shouldn't expect to be able to work full days. Jerry knew, because he had gone through a similar experience: He'd lost a son to murder twenty years earlier. He helped me know what to expect. I cried 150 times in 180 days, which is ten times more than I'd cried in my whole life. He helped me give myself grace for that. He told me it would be about a year before I'd get back to 90 percent, and he was right."

Leaning on a team was a huge part of that. Steve says, "I quickly realized that if Tricia and I were going to hold on to our marriage, I'd have to learn to look past my own pain. I was told the divorce rate for people who lose kids is 80 percent—50 percent for Christian families, which I don't think is much of an improvement."

Steve tells people that a major component to moving past his own pain was seeing God's grace in the blitz. Realistically, given the path they were following, Joel and his friend weren't on a track leading to successful lives. Joel, however, had recently made peace with God and reconciled with everyone in his life. In this, Steve and Tricia saw God's goodness and plan. Instead of choosing anger and victimization, they chose gratitude. Instead of isolation, they chose unity. They released their dreams for their family to God's transcendent plan, whatever that was, even though it didn't necessarily make sense to them. "I don't know why this happened," Tricia says, "but I don't really need to understand why. I know God, and I know He is good."

Accepting the Death of a Dream

I am a dreamer, a visionary, raised by a father who had huge visions and dreams. But let's be reminded: We can get ourselves too wrapped up in dreams. I'm not saying they're wrong. Incredible dedication to dreams is awesome. But when you attach your full identity, faith, and contentment to it, the dream becomes risky and dangerous for your own emotional well-being—not to mention your physical health, relationships, and more. Sometimes you just need to let that dream die and develop a new one, a more realistic one for right now.

Maybe the dreams should die because they were shallow dreams. They wouldn't have brought any more than temporary satisfaction anyway. They were rooted in your own selfish desires and idealistic picture of reality. They failed to embrace the bigger perspective and more realistic vision of being a generous person with loyal

50

relationships. What you really need is a dream that can be shared, that doesn't bankrupt your identity if it disappears.

For example, a dream of fame, wealth, and comfortable circumstances is based on *doing, performing,* and *having,* not being. Real success is based on *being.* Think about it. Are your dreams about investing in life, and lives, or about consuming? We'll talk more about that in upcoming chapters.

It wasn't a bad dream for me to want to be a successful quarterback. I wouldn't have been any good if I didn't have that dream. By the same token, if I had defined myself solely by the achievement of my dream, when the dream struggled or died, I would have lost myself.

When the loss happens, it's easy to lose your ability to be content and be your best self for your spouse, your kids, your friends, or your co-workers, regardless of the circumstances. That's why your identity needs to be something more than your dream of accomplishments. It needs to be who you are in belief, character, and relationships. You need a dream that is less transitory, less uncertain, and less conditional than what is found in the temporal circumstances of dream-achievement.

Losing the Dream Without Losing Yourself

Succumbing to the values of our performance-based, image-conscious society is all too natural. It can happen without thinking about it. We're imperfect people with insecurities. It's an easy thing to do, because we all tend to define ourselves by the way people view us, or by the way we *think* they view us.

But if we do that, if we define ourselves by the views others have of us, we then fall into the measurements and labels of popularity garnering, attention gathering, money making, points scoring, game winning, bonus earning, headline grabbing, and lifestyle impressing, to name a few. Many men and women wrap themselves up in trying to validate themselves physically, sexually, and

51

financially. When our identity is wrapped up in our achievements and status, all sorts of obsessions, imbalances, and greed result. Midlife identity crises often send guys chasing after fitness, sports, and women as though they were in high school all over again. And when we find that some of those things are less satisfying and more empty than anticipated, we go after something else. The chase has no end.

Women can feel and adopt all the same measures of identity and worth while adding the additional component of exaggerated beauty. They face the harsh societal mirror of unattainable and unsustainable beauty. They may also develop an unrealistic expectation of the ideal family. They may draw their identities from the other people to whom they relate, such as their children or husbands. Their identity becomes wrapped up in who they are in the context of these relationships, and they fail to cultivate a confidence and an identity in who they are as individuals. When the children leave home, they sometimes feel lost, and so do their lives.

There are some people who live without a strong sense of self, not because it's wrapped up in other people, but because it's never been validated. Their parents or families of origin didn't validate them, so maybe they looked for this in their workplaces. People who don't have a clearly defined sense of self may get a lot of extrinsic validation relationally in that work environment—and by finding their identity there may miss out on the deeper satisfaction of giving themselves selflessly in authentic, non-work-based relationships.

None of us will *ever* get our ultimate need for validation fully satisfied by what raise we received, what promotions we earned, what impressive circles we ran in, or what possessions, adventures, and club memberships we added to our achievement lists. Those things are all temporary and only partial validations of who we really are. And at the end of the day, if they're all we have, they will feel like counterfeits. When they fail, along with the dreams we have built around them, all too often our identity fails with them. This ought not to be; in fact, failure can be our needed friend if we let it!

Comedic celebrity commentator Conan O'Brien left his personal safety net to go after a bigger dream, but ultimately lost out on his hoped-for chance to take over *The Tonight Show*. Soon after that he gave a particularly self-disclosing commencement speech at my alma mater, Dartmouth College. He described his very public and embarrassing disappointment at not getting what he wanted, and watched his career journey off a path that he'd energetically forged.

But without a job or a navigation system, Conan tried fun, crazy new things, like tweeting comedy, playing guitar, doing stand-up and a national tour and a documentary. And through it all, he said that "something spectacular" unfolded.

> It was the most satisfying and fascinating year of my professional life. . . . I have never had more fun, been more challenged . . . and had more conviction about what I was doing. . . .
>
> There are few things more liberating in this life than having your worst fear realized. . . .
>
> It is our failure to become our perceived ideal that ultimately defines us and makes us unique. It's not easy, but if you accept your misfortune and handle it right, your perceived failure can be a catalyst for profound re-invention.[1]

Conan illustrates a key point. If we need to be going in a different direction, we usually need a catalyst—often cathartic—to get the ball rolling. Career changes after layoffs are a good example of this. Sometimes a relationship gets healed after we go through an illness, or a marriage is saved, or a new team is formed, a new business is launched, or . . .

. . . you just never know what God has in store.

Getting a Realistic Picture of You

To me, there are few people who exemplify this philosophy more than my buddy Tom Flick. Tom came from a large family, the younger brother of many athletic siblings. He went to college at the University of Washington and was a Rose Bowl quarterback who entered the NFL at the same time I did. After our retirements we became best friends.

Ironically, Tom had a rather quiet start in life. He was voted the shyest person in his high school, the least likely to stand up in front of a crowd. He wasn't an up-front kind of person at all. In fact, he pretty much put all his energies into his sports—which paid off because he became a great football player.

After being drafted into the NFL, Tom's career had numerous almost-but-just-didn't-happen experiences. He kept getting traded, eventually playing for five different teams in all, each with different offensive systems, different coaches, and different dynamics. He often found himself on losing teams.

When he was entering his eighth year in football, Tom's mother developed cancer. In response, Tom did the almost unimaginable: He walked away. Close to his family, and frustrated by what was going on in pro football, he set aside his dream and went home to help care for his ailing mother. This was of more value to him than pursuing his dream of a successful career in pro football.

It wasn't that Tom had failed. Circumstances simply hadn't allowed him to be on the right team with the right coach. So he played the hand he'd been dealt. He faced the blitz of his mother's illness, returned home to be with her, ended his football career, and never went back to it.

He didn't need to, because Tom embraced a bigger vision. He had a more comprehensive perspective of who he was and what he wanted to accomplish in life. Tom was able to let his football dream die because there was something more important to which he was loyal.

He began speaking to school children about character, virtues, and living a life of impact, about getting a good education and being a person of integrity. Over the next ten years, he who was voted least likely to speak in front of a crowd ended up communicating to over a million children, speaking hundreds of times a year!

Later, Tom felt impressed that he should transition from speaking to kids to speaking to businesses. At first he didn't think he had anything to say, but he did it anyway. Today, he's speaking fifty times a year to major corporations and enjoying a successful career built on helping others be the best they can be in unselfish, team-oriented ways.

Tom had a vision for something greater than his original dream, but he never would have found it if he hadn't been willing to let the original dream die.

The Difference Between a Dream and a Vision

What is a vision exactly? Vision is the meaning behind life, the long-term arc of your journey, the potential you see before it is realized. It's the comeback before you get up off the ground, the silver lining during the darkness of the storm, the positive change you create in your mind before you see it in your situation, the new way to do things before people realize the old way is inadequate or obsolete.

Helen Keller was deaf and blind, but she had incredible vision. She overcame what to most people would have been an insurmountable obstacle. She turned her blitz into an incredible life of impacting others. Among these were the students who heard her speeches. Her answer to a college student's question about what could be worse than being blind was an emphatic, "It would be so much worse to have eyesight but lack vision."

Vision is what the mother of a friend of mine saw in her little boy who, though he had dyslexia and endured more hardship and less success in school than most kids, was a boy with gifts and potential. He simply processed things differently. But that didn't stop him.

His parents determined he was worth the private schools and extra help they gave him. Jimmy grew up to do decently in high school, play football, and get into an Ivy League college. He tried out for the New England Patriots and didn't make the team—which was a hope dashed—yet he persevered. He carried the vision his mother had planted in his heart: *You're smart. You can learn. You WILL be successful.* His education got him a job as an architect, gave him a visual of the world, and his architectural firm became very successful. He was the best man at my wedding. To this day he's a successful man in his family and is designing homes of excellence.

This sort of vision, the kind demonstrated by Helen Keller, by my friend Tom, and by Jimmy's parents, is what helps you recover from the loss of a dream. A *dream* is rooted in one set of circumstances and is often self-focused. A *vision*, on the other hand, has a much broader perspective.

Dreams are often our goals, our plan of where we want to be, in circumstance, achievement, and reputation. Martin Luther King Jr.'s dream was really a vision because it wasn't just for him—it was so much bigger than that. It was for change in the way people saw and valued each other, how they behaved together, and how society's prejudices could be erased in time.

Finding That Bigger Vision

Reality must be faced. We are not what we do, whom we work for, or who the public sees us to be. We're persons with spirits, souls, personalities, emotions, stories, wounds, fears, virtues, strengths, and weaknesses. To understand these things about ourselves is to know ourselves. We become free to live at peace with others, to live with contentment not dependent on circumstances, and to handle the losses in life—including the loss of certain dreams.

Steve Jobs got fired from Apple. Conan lost *The Tonight Show.* All of us lose things we desperately wanted. I lost my chance to become a long-term starter in the NFL. But I didn't lose my identity. I didn't tank; I stayed valuable to the team, utilized my platform to be of help to other players and their wives, and made my off-the-field life count. Eventually I had to face the loss of my career at age thirty-three with my release from the Philadelphia Eagles. There, my self-definition as a professional athlete ended, along with the quest to achieve goals, win a championship, and get a new contract.

The loss of a dream—like not reaching your original goal in life—is successfully survived by embracing a vision that includes a bigger picture: new opportunities, valued relationships, and helping others, even if you cannot attain the circumstances you desire. The loss of a dream or failure of a life goal is converted to good when you turn your sights to lifting others, using your pain to learn from your disappointment and help people. Think long term. Be willing to change. Focus on loving and lifting others.

Time Out for Self-Reflection

In the introduction I asked three questions that determine whether we practice the three strategies for beating life's blitzes. They represent the perspective on life and the power to live out these requirements. This chapter on embracing a bigger vision is the right time to sharpen our focus by seeing things through these three lenses:

Do you see life as an individual sport or a team sport?

Do you look at the world from the stand-point of a consumer or an investor?

What is your power source?

These questions invite you to question and counter the normal way society sees things. They are countercultural. They're not the popular and natural way to live in a society that sells lifestyles and magazines with the title *Self*. We live in a me-centered culture. *My* entitlements. *My* rights. *My* personal happiness and satisfaction.

The three lenses offer a much different perspective. Teamwork. Investing in others. Connecting to a trustworthy power source.

These are three vital lenses to gain a bigger vision. They give us a clearer look at life in order to face and overcome our blitzes. They are foundations upon which to build our lives, and our best response to troubles, trials, and temptations.

Take a few minutes to answer the following questions:

- What are my life lenses?
- In what situations do I take a team approach, and in what situations do I take a solo approach? What practical things can I do to adopt a team approach?
- When is my mind-set like a consumer's and when is it like an investor's?
- What do I need to do more of to be an investor, especially in other people?
- What is my power source? Is it dependable? Is it enough? Am I connected?

Developing a Life Vision

The personal philosophy I have embraced is this: With a realistic humility about my inherent imperfection, *I have incredible worth to the God who created me.* His love defines my significance, and my life is meant to be an encouragement and support to others. And at the end of the day, no success will satisfy me if I can't share it with other people, especially with my wife and family.

I've also developed a life vision or mission statement that has helped me articulate, define, and aim my life more specifically. I encourage you to do the same. Take some time to think about and write down

1. What has been most important to you in the past?
2. What do you want to be most important to you in the future?
3. Who do you most want to help in life, and how do you want to help them?

58

4. What is your greatest strength, the sweet spot of how you make life better for others and enjoyable for yourself?

5. What are five dominant ways you're spending your time, in order of actual allocation?

6. What are the top five ways, in order of priority, you'd *want* to spend your time?

Run the Play: Practical Application

1. From your observations, create a three- to five-sentence mission statement articulating your vision and priorities for your life.

2. Post this somewhere you can see it regularly as a reminder for vision and inspiration.

3. TIP: If this doesn't come easily to you, ask God for help. His desires for our lives are better than our own. Ask for ideas and settle in to listen. Then write down what comes into your heart and mind. You may also ask a mentor-like friend for help, to listen to you and help you to synthesize and write down what you say.

4. Consider deeply the suffering, death, and resurrection of Jesus. In light of this, how can you change your attitude about the losses, setbacks, and troubles in your life?

Sample Life Vision

Here's a sample life vision, my personal mission statement. Yours can be longer or shorter. You can use bullet points or even diagrams if you think better in those formats.

- My highest priority in life is to intentionally love and uplift my God, my wife, and my family.

- I want God's presence and love to fuel my life so that I may lift and unite other people to invest in relationships, teamwork, and family.

- I want to help people see marriage for what it is—the ultimate team, the DNA of civilization, and the epitome of teamwork that allows us to become our better selves and serve a cause greater than ourselves.
- I want to help men find and fulfill their identity and mission as men—built for others—to protect women and children, raise boys to manhood, and commit to marriage and family.
- I will team with caring, talented, others-centered people to help others experience a connected and uplifting life, the kind of life received from God and shared with others.

Be Willing to Change

> Take a Deep, Honest Look at Yourself
> Cultivate a Relational Value System
> Be an Investor, Not a Consumer

4

Take a Deep, Honest Look at Yourself

*You must take personal responsibility. You cannot
change the circumstances, the seasons, or the wind,
but you can change yourself.*

Jim Rohn

I was the starting quarterback for the Seattle Seahawks in 1991
when we lost an important game against Kansas City. In my
quotes to reporters after the game, I chose not to dwell on the
loss or my own personal failings. Instead, I played the role of an
optimist and said, "We're going to do better next week; we're
going to turn the corner and go forward."

Later that week, one of my teammates, Eugene Robinson, a
close friend and great defensive player, came to me privately and
said, "Dude, a bunch of the coaches and defensive guys are questioning whether you're a stand-up guy or an excuse maker. They
don't think you're owning up to your responsibility for that loss."

Having my character questioned slammed me harder than looking at a dismal quarterback rating or even being booed by the
crowd. This criticism was aimed right at who I was—my character.

I felt like I was under an avalanche of emotional attack, and it really, *really* bothered me.

The NFL is a feast-or-famine world of little security and even less stability. Because of the way I'd handled the postgame interview, a number of my coaches and teammates thought I had completely failed as a starter. They thought that, in my optimism, I'd left the blame with the team instead of taking my part in it. Not only had I contributed to the loss, it seemed I wasn't being an accountable and trustworthy leader.

I felt misread and misjudged. I decided to talk privately to a couple of the defensive coaches who reportedly held these concerns. I told them I was my own worst critic and knew I'd fallen way short of what we needed to win. I knew I'd played a major role in our loss. My eyes misted up as I conveyed to them how much it hurt that coaches and teammates didn't feel I had taken responsibility for my losing performance.

They knew I was sincere and it ended well. But my sons and I still talk about this story when discussing the importance of leaders taking responsibility—even taking the fall—after an error or failure. If a team falters or multiple people fall short, you've got to focus on *your* part of things first.

My team wanted to hear that I understood my role in our loss. My play wasn't the only reason we lost, but they needed to see that, first, I got it, and second, I was willing to take the heat, not simply leave it with my teammates and coaches.

Why Take Responsibility?

What I'm about to say might sound foolish in a land filled with lawyers, but the reality is that taking the blame improves relationships, even if your screw-up was a minor percentage of what went wrong. Let's face it: If you don't take the blame for your own mistakes, other people will spend their time, effort, and energy accusing you.

Taking the blame brings about several good things:

First, it motivates you. You work even harder to fix the mistakes you made, because you've voiced them to others. Everybody knows that *you* know what went wrong and why, and they heard you affirm you were going to do something about it.

Second, accepting responsibility sets a good example. People are more willing to admit to their own mistakes and take responsibility for them after seeing you've done the same. Once they see you admitting to your faults, they feel safer admitting their own. Someone needs to lead the healing by facing the truth first.

Third, people are more likely to defend you if you're not the one defending yourself. If you deny any role in what went wrong, your teammates, co-workers, or family members are liable to spend their energy pointing out what they think you did wrong rather than spend their energy defending you, forgiving you, or examining their own roles in the matter.

My friend Todd Peterson was an excellent NFL kicker for the Seahawks. Todd rarely missed field goals, but in one game he missed a much-needed kick. In postgame interviews, Todd expressed his self-disappointment, though he also hinted that a poor snap and hold of the ball had contributed to the miss. Former Seahawk star and assistant coach Jim Zorn pulled Todd aside and explained to him that coaches like to defend a player, but they can't do that unless the player takes undiluted responsibility for his actions rather than defending himself or calling out others to share the blame. Todd took the advice to heart; he was a model of integrity and service to others throughout his NFL career and today.

Staying focused on that partial, or even minor, percentage in which you failed helps you to improve and gives you credibility. We've seen many examples of celebrities, CEOs, and politicians who had public failings and immediately went into spin-and-containment control with their PR teams. They focused on being defensive instead of quickly coming clean, apologizing with sincerity, and admitting what they did wrong. Doesn't this always make the problem seem worse? Responsibility means taking the blame. It doesn't water it down or divvy the blame up for others.

Examine Yourself First

Once, I was leading a group of men in a short class on being a good husband when a buddy in the group shared a story that packed a powerful lesson. It's a lesson for all of us to live—men, women, married or single—in our relationships, our families, and our vocations.

An acquaintance of his was a good guy, a dutiful family man who unfortunately drifted out of balance in his life. He became super busy at work, was devotedly coaching Little League, and filled the rest of his schedule as a Boy Scout leader. Guess who wasn't feeling much of his love?

His wife.

One day this man came home from work early and found his wife in bed with one of his best friends. He was shocked and horrified. They were humiliated. But when his shock and disgust cooled a bit, he did something we rarely do when facing life-crushing moments—he looked inside himself. He asked himself, *What allowed my wife to fall out of love with me and into the arms of another man? How could things go so wrong in our marriage that she'd turn to an affair with my friend? What have I done or not done that allowed her to fall away from me?*

This husband realized he had gotten so busy choosing other things—good things, to be sure—that he'd neglected to choose the best thing: his wife. He'd gotten so carried away with competing pursuits that he hadn't been cherishing his wife, hadn't been valuing her and meeting her needs, hadn't been *loving* her. Instead, he'd been placing other priorities over her, so that she was no longer secure in his love. Finally she drifted from him and succumbed to temptation.

Amazingly, it was this scandalously wronged husband who was the one to go back to his wife, humbling himself and initiating an apology. He asked her to forgive him. "I've been wrong," he said. "I haven't cared for you. I've been too busy paying attention to other things and not you. I let you fall out of love with me."

He *wasn't* saying that what she did was defensible or that it hadn't hurt him. It *devastated* him. But he realized he'd taken his love from her and, in that regard, had let her down. He came to the painful conclusion that his wife never would have had an affair if he'd paid more attention to her, made her more of a priority, and loved her as she needed to be loved.

His apology melted his wife's lonely, hurt, and guilt-ridden heart. She, in turn, apologized to him and to the others she had hurt. She was able to apologize to God too and feel her Creator's forgiveness, just as she'd felt her husband's forgiveness. Then she and her husband began the hard work of putting their marriage back together.

Most couples in similar circumstances attack and blame each other instead of reflecting on their own shortcomings and trying to learn from them. When they do that, they rarely survive as a couple. But because this man turned the mirror on himself *first*, this brutal blitz became a wake-up call from which he and his wife could recover.

Today, this man's marriage is deeper, more intimate, and more transparent after having sustained a terrible blitz that none of us would ever want to go through. Against the odds, honesty and humility allowed him and his wife to build a new marriage—more honest, intentional, and prioritized than before their crisis. A better marriage than before the blitz.

Love sees the big picture, takes the long-term view. It's also humble. Humility sees beyond the weaknesses, faults, and failings of others to the good that lies within—knowing that we too have similar faults and failings within us. As Jesus said: "Don't point out and pluck out the speck in someone else's eye until you've pulled the log out of your own"[1] (my paraphrase). You've got to start with *yourself.*

The Power of Self-Reflection

We all face blitzes. You may know right now exactly what your blitz is . . . or you're still in the middle of it. Or maybe you're still reeling from a blitz in your past. You're still recovering or need to begin recovering. Or it may be that you don't immediately recognize what your blitzes are or have been. You've been coping, hiding, or denying. You're forging ahead with your head down and your foot on the pedal. You're busy. You haven't dealt with some big things in your past.

When my friend and former Seahawk teammate Steve Largent was young, his dad abandoned the family. Steve grew up without connection to his biological father. That was hard enough. But the blitz only worsened when his father eventually did contact Steve, who by now was a professional football player, and all his father wanted was tickets to a game. That only added to the injury, pain, and anger. Steve admitted, "I wrote it off, completely closed myself off emotionally to my dad, and put it in a box where I wouldn't have to deal with it."

Eventually, Steve realized he needed to take responsibility for his relationship with his father, insofar as it lay with him, and try to reconcile. Sure, it would have been easy—and justifiable—to point the finger at his dad for the abandonment and disappointment he'd felt over the years. Yet Steve chose to look at himself first and take ownership for the ways *he* had contributed to the chasm between them.

Steve contacted his father and apologized for the ways he hadn't been a good son, for not being more open toward his dad. Steve's humility softened his father's heart, and they formed a reconciliation of sorts. The extra payoff for Steve was that his relationship with his father was no longer a debilitating, ongoing blitz. By reflecting on his own responses and responsibility, he made himself less a victim of the original offense and became part of the solution. He let himself out of a box of pain and brought closure to his blitz.

Self-reflection is a powerful tool. For the couple whose blitz was an affair, self-reflection—turning the mirror on oneself first—wasn't a one-time act. They *kept* self-reflecting. Each had to identify what errors he or she had made as an individual so they would never allow something like this to happen to them again.

The message here isn't that an affair can strengthen your marriage or that apologizing will erase the pain of an offense. Even today, I imagine they both really wish the affair had never happened. Rather, the message is that *good can come from bad. There is always hope. We can learn and grow.* We can use a shocking and painful blitz to take us to new places, to deeper levels of honesty, humility, and maturity.

God's Take on Blitzes

Maybe you're not sure where you are spiritually. Perhaps you have some big doubts or some anger toward God. You have questions but you don't want to be preached at. I have you in mind as I write this. I'd like to briefly introduce a radical view of life's blitzes, with a transcending purpose and hope behind our experiences with losses, trials, and troubles.

We humans like to figure things out on our own, but that can cause us to miss so much of the big picture. If we are created beings, it would make sense to learn from the Creator. God's perspective on blitzes is very personal. It is demonstrated in how Jesus Christ lived, died, and came to life again. This is the Son of God, God in human form, the only perfect person in history. He came to blind and crippled people. He came to people who were morally wrecked, ostracized by others. He turned their physical pain and social suffering into positives, not just for them, but for the crowds who witnessed what He did. He healed them physically. More important, He healed them spiritually. Jesus forgave their sins and set them free to live differently. He turned bad into good.

Personally, Jesus knew He would face the most horrific and ultimate blitz. He told His twelve disciples what would happen, He faced it head on, and it turned out to be the ultimate triumph in history.

Jesus turned the worst into the best—He's the ultimate model for beating the blitz. He focused on the eternal purpose of God. He left the realm of heaven to become a human (an infant even). He gave himself for others (for us!). He depended upon His Father's power. He who was crucified and rose to life again is the definitive authority on facing troubles, trials, and affliction . . . on loss, suffering, and tribulation . . . on blitzes.

Jesus predicted blitzes for us as well. He told us, "In this world you will have trouble. But take heart! I have overcome the world" (John 16:33).

> I have told you these things, so that in Me you may have [perfect] peace and confidence. In the world you have tribulation and trials and distress and frustration; but be of good cheer [take courage; be confident, certain, undaunted]! For I have overcome the world. [I have deprived it of power to harm you and have conquered it for you.]
>
> John 16:33 AMP

There is no pretending we'll live trouble-free lives. On the contrary, the Bible warns us that blitzes will come, and it gives us the strategy for what to do. The apostle Paul communicated much of that strategy.

Paul was qualified to coach us on blitzes. As a young, zealous Jewish lawyer, he initially hated Jesus. He opposed the earliest disciples until God blinded him and Jesus appeared to him. Suddenly he believed and was radically transformed. That blitz set him on a life course that ultimately changed the world. Paul faced extreme opposition, shipwrecks, illnesses, beatings, and imprisonments.

From prison he penned many of the God-inspired words in the New Testament that illuminate God's instruction on facing life's blitzes. He wrote a letter to the early believers in Jesus who were meeting together in Rome, explaining the unsurpassable gift God gives to all those who believe in Jesus as their Savior. He said they are no longer separate from God, but intimate with Him because of what Jesus endured and accomplished for them; they have been given complete forgiveness and peace that will last forever. They will share God's life forever and share in His glory. He celebrates this as their preeminent cause to rejoice and exult.

> *Therefore, having been justified by faith, we have peace with God through our Lord Jesus Christ, through whom also we have obtained our introduction by faith into this grace in which we stand; and we exult in hope of the glory of God.*
>
> Romans 5:1–2 NASB

As Paul discusses blitzes (well, sans the football jargon), he uses similar language about rejoicing and exulting. He lays out the strategy and value of facing life's hits, trials, and tribulations.

As you look at this continuation of Paul's letter, don't be afraid to substitute the word *blitz* for *tribulation*.

> *And not only this, but we also exult in our tribulations, knowing that tribulation brings about perseverance; and perseverance, proven character; and proven character, hope; and hope does not disappoint, because the love of God has been poured out within our hearts through the Holy Spirit who was given to us.*
>
> Romans 5:3–5 NASB

Wait. Play that back. This seems bizarre. Is it just fuzzy spiritual talk? Heavenly minded, but no good in real life?

It's saying we should exult and rejoice, be positive and grateful for the hard, painful, and tragic things in life we all hope to avoid. That's paradoxical. It definitely has eternity in mind, spiritual and heavenly things. But it is also practical, everyday, real-life wisdom.

It goes like this: No one deserves the forgiveness, healed relationship, and eternal life that God has given us because of the blitz Jesus faced for us, yet God gives us ultimate and never-ending joy, and we celebrate that.

But we also celebrate and thank God for the hard stuff. Tribulations cause us to take our eyes off temporary circumstances and fading earthly comforts. They remind us to relate to God, depend on Him and persevere through Him. That perseverance in relationship and dependence on God causes our character to change. We become more like Jesus, with proven character that perfectly balances faith, truth, and love, because our vision is set on eternal life with God. Being more like Jesus with that eternal vision gives us what this world is desperate to find: hope. And this hope is real because Jesus loved us, died for us, and lives forever. God's Spirit gives us that amazing love, which we don't deserve and can't earn.

Trials and tribulations, losses and injuries redirect us from seeking our satisfaction from our circumstances. In turning to God for help and hope, we realize even more how much we are loved. More troubles on earth . . . more love from God.

This is a radical view of troubles, trials, and tribulations in this life. We rejoice in them. We're grateful for them. Why? Because we know that facing hardship drives us to pursue a relationship with Jesus, to depend on Him and persevere by trusting Him, not ourselves or our circumstances. Persevering in Christ changes our character, heightens our hope in eternal salvation, and deepens our experience of God's love.

God's goal is not our comfort. It's much bigger and better than that. It is His glory. His glory is love. His love, which prompts our love for Him and for one another, is God's glory. Consider how quick we are to seek comfort, control, and significance in our circumstances in life instead of in our relationship to God.

Think through the chapters of your life and how exulting in Christ during suffering, rejoicing in troubles, and positively facing your trials would change life for you, as well as for those around you. God urges us to prepare for blitzes.

He invites us to trust and turn to Christ in our troubles. We'll become more like Jesus, more eternity-focused and others-centered. Enduring with Christ wins His approval. We experience more of His love as we focus on Jesus, not our circumstances. It's a radical and powerful invitation: Face your blitzes through

Jesus, who gives you strength, hope, and love. God is with us in our most brutal moments and gut-wrenching experiences. He is there in our disappointments and frustrations. God has suffered more than we have, and Jesus overcame death so we can overcome any blitz, including death. He won't force himself on us, though. We need to turn to Jesus and let Him love us, change us, and guide our lives.

Time Out for Self-Reflection

Apply what you learned in this chapter to the roles you play in the different spheres of your life. Where have you encountered a blitz? Think about

- Family of origin
- Childhood relationships and school
- Sports and athletics
- College and career experiences
- On the job/business
- Romantic relationships and marriage
- Children
- Friendships, faith community, neighbors
- Accidents and injuries
- Health

Write down one self-reflective thought for each area where you've experienced a blitz, trial, or setback. What is one thing you can name that is your OWN responsibility, either in contributing to or responding to that blitz?

(Remember, this doesn't apply to conflicts and trials initiated by childhood abuse, neglect, abandonment, bullying, or verbal, psychological, or sexual abuse or rape. If these have been issues for you, I encourage you to include a therapist, counselor, or faith leader/pastor into your reflection and healing process.)

Run the Play: Practical Application

Take one action. Visit or call one person to improve your response to a blitz. Don't revisit the whole blitz and what may have happened to you, but examine where you have erred or fallen short in your response. Ask the person to forgive you for your attitude or for not treating them with the respect or the kindness you'd like.

5

Cultivate a Relational Value System

Those who are happiest are those who do the most for others.

Booker T. Washington, *Up from Slavery*

In the mid-1980s, I was playing for the Los Angeles Rams when I had the opportunity to volunteer with the Special Olympics at UCLA as a "celebrity helper." It was my first exposure to the Special Olympics, a place where love and competition meet in a beautiful celebration of the best in the human spirit. I'll never forget the 100-meter dash where in every lane, at the finish line, stood a "hugger."

What's a hugger?

It's a volunteer who's there waiting at the end of the race for the young athletes to finish. As these uniquely challenged and gifted people run down the lanes—some fast, some slow, some distracted and waving to the people on the sidelines—their personal huggers cheer them on. When the runners cross the finish line, the huggers are ready with huge celebratory hugs and words of encouragement.

"You looked great."

"You were super!"

"Way to go!"

"I love to watch you run."

Wouldn't it be great if there were huggers in all areas of life?

I'm not saying the sports world doesn't need vigorous competition and the passionate drive for victory. Of course it does, as does the marketplace and a number of other fields that depend on hard work, excellence, and achievement. Here's the point: *relationally*, the experience of the athletes and huggers at the Special Olympics stands out markedly from what I experienced in pro football, and even from what most of us experienced in junior high school. It's worlds apart from what we see on reality TV shows like *The Bachelor* and *The Bachelorette*, on Wall Street, and in much of the marketplace. For the most part, it is a *conditional, performance-based value system* dominating those arenas. Winners get picked, while others get compared, judged, and rejected.

Comparison.

So many of our blitzes in life come from being criticized, sidelined, or rejected by people and organizations. The conditional, performance-based value system grinds us up and spits us out.

Competition.

"What have you done for me *lately*?"

"What are you *worth to me*?"

Yet for those Special Olympians, it was a great feeling simply to run, apart from whether or not they won. They felt valued independently of whether they were the first or the last one to cross that finish line. Really, that's an awesome feeling for *all* of us, isn't it—when it happens? There's something very powerful, and very needed, about being validated, not for what you do but simply for who you are.

Discovering a Transcendent Value System

After my experience of being benched and demoted two spots in the '88 game between the Seahawks and the 49ers, I felt as if my last chance to succeed had come and gone. I'd realized by this time how little sense it made to reject people relationally when their performance or marketplace worth diminished. I'd gained some experience and perspective the hard way. It was the most brutal chapter of my career, but one that helped to shape my life vision and future value system. Eventually my hope and confidence rebounded, revitalized by a transcendent value system quite different from the one I'd been encountering.

> Strange is our situation here upon earth. Each of us comes for a short visit, not knowing why, yet sometimes seeming to divine a purpose. From the standpoint of daily life, however, there is one thing we do know: that man is here for the sake of other men.
>
> Albert Einstein

Facing failure, demotions, and rejections in football helped me to gain another crucial perspective: My relationship with a person should not be based on how well I like his or her external packaging and status. *What's his performance on the field? What does she look like? What has she accomplished? How much money does he have? How successful is he? How popular is she?*

These conditional valuations are corrosive if they sum up how we view people. They make kids so insecure that they're afraid to make friends. They make teenagers take risks and shortcuts, hoping to be accepted. They make adults so insecure that they take ethical shortcuts and make moral compromises. When people don't know their inherent worth and value, when they only know a conditional value system, they often sacrifice marriage, family, faith, and ethics on the altar of success, popularity, or acceptance. But it's an effort in vain. There is little true success apart from character, faith, and family. Integrity and relationships are the currency of being at peace, enjoying life.

Clearly, performance and competition are central to human advancement and epic achievements. Rewards and incentives have their specific value. But none of these things intrinsically enhances or demeans the value of an individual. Likewise, winning is important, in its place. I'm pretty sure it's not "the only thing," as Vince Lombardi once declared, but winning is definitely a vital goal. Doesn't it feel good to have someone hug you, to affirm you, to love you regardless of whether you've won or lost—to value you for who you are and not for what you've done, for your *relationship* and not just for your *performance*?

Adopting Relational Values

Do you know that nothing you do in this life will ever matter, unless it is about loving God and loving the people He has made?

Francis Chan

My son Keegan reminded me of the difference between a performance-based and relationally based value system when at age five he was shooting baskets with me in our backyard. The ball was huge in his little hands, and he was uncorking his whole body to shoot the ball ten feet up to make a basket. Despite his full-out effort, he just couldn't get the big basketball all the way past the rim and into the basket. Undaunted, with a wide smile on his face, and even though he hadn't sunk a single shot, he turned to me and said confidently, "Daddy, I'm good at the shootin' part. I'm just not good at the makin' part!"

I chuckled at his creative distinction between shooting and making shots. His tempered confidence and humility over the "not good at the makin' part" only endeared him to me even more. It was one of those poignant moments you know you're going to remember for the rest of your life. I loved him like crazy. I was so grateful for and thrilled by him at that moment, and I am to this day.

My love for Keegan wasn't based on his skill at shooting or his percentage of shots made. Yet, through the course of our lives, it becomes more difficult for most of us to avoid treating people on a conditional and performance basis, including those most valuable to us, like our spouses and children. Society and its ways rub off on us more than we realize. It's important to step back, examine ourselves, and realize the difference between the culture and our best desires.

Why do most of us drift away from a relationally based value system? Why don't we view people through a relational lens, like the way I was viewing Keegan that day? All too often we look at other people through standards of performance, appearance, and economics. It's conditional—and we assume they're measuring us the same way.

Stop for a minute and do a self-check. Is your own value system, when it comes to evaluating *yourself*, based on relational or performance-based criteria? To find out just where you may be on the relational vs. performance scale, ask yourself the following:

- Do I beat myself up when I don't measure up or succeed?
- How conditional am I about my identity? Is my sense of who I am affected by what I own, what I do, or who I'm with?
- Is my sense of self-worth based on circumstances, which by definition are subject to change?

Now think about the standard by which you evaluate and treat *others*:

- When you're at a party or social gathering, what guides you in choosing who you want to talk to or be with? Do you think about how you can offer kindness to or interest in other people? Or do you think about who is impressive, attractive, or accomplished, hoping to be around them more than others?
- Does your treatment of your friends vary depending on their successes or failures? What are you like at work, with peers, bosses, and those you supervise? Do you stay warm and relationally interested when you are corrected, or when you need to correct others when their performance lags?
- Sadly, we often take the people closest to us for granted, our family and those in our own home. Does your spouse see you

as a relational person whose love is unconditional, or do they experience you as a performance-oriented and conditional person? How about your children . . . with grades, clothes, hair, sports, etc?

- Asking tough questions is good for us. Do you value performance first or the person first? If a person doesn't perform, impress, or add value in your eyes, do you still care about that person?

If you're up for digging a little deeper, think back throughout your life and see if you can trace back the development of your value system. Ask yourself

- Who in my life treated me with a *conditional* value system, where my worth and acceptance were based on how well I performed?
- Who treated me with an *unconditional* value system, where I was loved and accepted regardless of how well I performed?
- How did each of these kinds of evaluations leave me feeling?

The Role of True Love

If you can't do great things, Mother Teresa used to say, do little things with great love. If you can't do them with great love, do them with a little love. If you can't do them with a little love, do them anyway. Love grows when people serve.

John Ortberg, *The Me I Want to Be: Becoming God's Best Version of You*

The relational value system that transcends a conditional, performance-based approach is rooted in love. Love is so much more than just a romantic notion. Love, in its essence, is a deep sense of caring for other human beings. Love is a verb. It's decisions and actions. Love means choosing, not just having feelings. It means to

80

will the best and do the best for others. People all through history have experienced and modeled love—people from thousands of cultural and religious backgrounds, from millions of family and sociological backgrounds. Yet love as a sacrificial and unconditional action, generous and self-giving, is not the ever-visible norm in most societies or in our personal experiences. Sadly, Hollywood, among other messengers, has left us somewhat confused and misguided on this point. And our most important relationships—at home and at work—have suffered as a result.

True love, if it exists, must come from somewhere. Have you ever thought about that? Where do *you* think it comes from?

Christian faith and the Scriptures describe a Creator God in a triune relationship of love between a Father, a Son, and a Holy Spirit. Jewish faith and the Torah point to a Father and the Messiah/Son He will send for His people. Each aspect and personality of God honors, uplifts, and cooperates perfectly with the others. The relationship between these aspects of God is a beautiful portrait for us of true love, the kind of love that sacrifices generously, seeking nothing in return. It's *unconditional* love.

There's a Jewish legend, often attributed to the Talmud, that illustrates this kind of love between two brothers:

> Once upon a time in the land of Israel, there lived an old farmer. When he died, the farmer left his land to his two sons. They divided the land evenly and built their own houses on opposite sides. The younger brother soon married and had a family. The older brother did not marry but lived alone. Both brothers remained the best of friends and often helped each other on their farms.
>
> One year at harvest time, both brothers undertook the process of harvesting their crops of barley. They bundled the stalks of grain into sheaves, counted them, and took them into their barns to store. (Later, they would take some of it to the market to sell.) After a long day of work, the brothers usually slept well. But on this night, the elder brother lay awake.
>
> *It is not right,* he thought, *that I should reap as much grain as my brother. He has a family to feed and I have only myself.*

81

He needs more barley to sell so that he can buy all that he needs for his family. Making up his mind to set things right, he dressed and slipped out to his barn. There he took as many sheaves as he could carry across the field to his brother's barn. Feeling better, he returned to his bed and slept well.

The younger brother also had slept badly that night. He awoke and lay worrying. He too thought of his brother. *It is not right,* he thought, *that I should reap as much grain as my brother. I have a family to help me and to care for me in old age, while he works alone.* He then rose, dressed, and went to his barn, not long after his brother had left. There he took as many sheaves as he could carry and walked across the field to his brother's barn. Feeling better, he returned to his bed.

The next day the two brothers each went to their barns. They looked and looked again at their grain. There was as much in their barns as had been there the day before. The two brothers worked again in their fields all day and did not speak of what had happened.

The next night they did the same thing. First, the older brother, taking as many sheaves of grain as he could carry to his brother's barn, and then the younger brother, narrowly missing him, did the same. Again, the next day both brothers stood in awe and counted their grain, which was as much as before they had given it away. Again, both kept their thoughts to themselves.

Then on the third night, both brothers rose late. The moon had gone down, and they went to their barns. Again they gathered as much grain as they could carry and headed across the field to the other brother's barn.

It was so dark that they almost collided in the middle of the field. They both stopped and stared at each other. What they saw made them smile, and then laugh. They dropped their bundles and hugged each other for a long, long time. They promised each other that there would always be help for each other, no matter what. Then they each knelt down right there in the field and thanked God for giving them such a thoughtful and generous brother.[1]

Love is not looking for an immediate return. It's looking at the long term. Love initiates, and love is not conditional. Love sacrifices.

But God shows and clearly proves His own love for us by the fact that while we were still sinners, Christ (the Messiah, the Anointed One) died for us.

Romans 5:8 AMP

Not-So-Valuable Approaches to People

There are multiple conditional and consumer-like ways of measuring people, including (but not limited to):

Performance

Popularity

Power

Possessions

Positions

Performance: You evaluate people based on how well they accomplish, achieve, and produce. Do they help you, impress you, or gratify you? You accept or reject them relative to how they "score" on a point system. It's a scorecard in your head, a way to either accept or reject people based on your ranking system.

Popularity: You value people based on their image and on how many others like them. If other people deem them attractive, interesting, or favorable, so do you. It's based on who you know and who knows you. Cliques, the "in crowd," and fame matter.

Power: You value people because of their positions of authority, influence, and privilege. You like being near the power, hoping that influence can benefit you. It shapes who you care about.

Possessions: You evaluate what people own and the impressiveness of the lifestyle they have. Their homes, cars, and "toys" influence your view of others and how you value them.

Positions: You value people by the degree to which they agree with you and your beliefs. You reject them if they fail your crucial test of aligning with your position on an issue or stance that you value over people. This is a case of wanting to be *right* more than wanting to be in *relationship*.

We all know there are times that we operate in these ways. But these shallow measures of people can work against developing healthy, lasting relationships.

Now, having a relational value system does not mean you become like a marshmallow or a doormat. It doesn't mean that competition, performance, and results are ignored, and that rewards, consequences, and penalties are not needed. It doesn't mean that if someone's performance is poor or a principle is compromised, you're obligated to give them the same treatment as before. That's not what I'm saying at all. That wouldn't be honest and true.

Here's the point: *Relationship ought not to be rejected and human value diminished because of external aspects of a person.* We need to face truth and speak truth, but we need to do it from a motivation of love, with a demeanor of respect and kindness.

Prioritizing a relationship doesn't mean a person can't be corrected. A relational value system influences HOW a person is corrected, not WHETHER. It also means the correction will probably be received better. It doesn't mean a person can't be fired; it means the firing will be done with more dignity and respect, and in a way that preserves the future for that person and improves the morale of the people who remain in the organization. It doesn't mean you can't bench a player for performing poorly; it means you have the best chance of keeping that player engaged for the next time he or she is called upon, for the benefit of the whole team.

Ruben Rodriguez was a talented young punter for the Seattle Seahawks who made the unfortunate error of punting a ball directly off the side of his foot into the sidelines, costing the team forty yards of field position. His special teams coach blew a gasket and began screaming at the top of his lungs, cusswords and all, directed straight at Ruben. Poor Ruben, a new NFL player, stepped off the field humiliated and wanting to hide. That was hard to do, since no one wanted to stand next to him.

Knowing how he felt, I walked up next to him, patted him on the back, and said, "It's all right. You'll be okay, Ruben." Unfortunately, I spoke a bit too loudly and ended up in the line of fire myself.

"It is not [BLEEPING] all right!" the coach yelled.

Now, I have to admit the special teams coach was correct, objectively speaking. It's *not* okay for players to make errors like that, for it hurts the team. But my perspective was that since he needed to kick a few more times that game and in future games, he should be in enough of a recovered frame of mind that he could continue to punt well. I wanted him to understand that while, admittedly, he had screwed up, he—the person—was still valued.

Results and relationships both matter deeply, but relationships ought to transcend, outlast, and support results. Emotional and relationship intelligence sees the value of people in an unconditional manner. It understands that relational investment is also the best pathway to better long-term and lasting performance and results.

The Role of ERQ vs. IQ

Contrary to what people might think, a relational value system is the one that promotes the most success in the business world. The research and work of David Olson and Gary Oliver (and Daniel Goleman and others) indicate that those who succeed today in leadership are not the people with the highest IQ, but rather those with the highest ERQ—Emotional Relational Quotient.

We're not talking about the *intelligence* quotient here, but the emotional and relational quotient, which Dr. Oliver defines as "The ability to be aware of, recognize and understand our own emotions and those of others and to constructively manage those emotions in ourselves and in our personal and professional relationships."[2]

This significantly increases our intrapersonal and interpersonal effectiveness and helps us initiate and maintain healthy and successful relationships. The great news is that, unlike IQ, which is largely genetic, ERQ can be cultivated and dramatically improved with consistent effort and application throughout our lives. It's never too late to increase your ERQ.

With that in mind, let's put a few pieces of human and organizational behavior together. Great organizations, teams, and businesses are those that create consistently excellent results for their customers and their own people. They create a culture of trust, loyalty, and dedication. Excellence and innovation result. They have a long-term perspective and shape a legacy. They value people, because it is people who accept and steward a lasting legacy. They are led by leaders of vision, focus, and humility. Humility and dogged focus on the vision are the vital traits found in "Level Five leaders," as Jim Collins discovered in his book *Good to Great*.[3] Great organizations focus on results *and* relationships, as Ken Blanchard and Mark Miller point out in *The Secret*.[4] The ultimate success—with results—of these organizations begins with the essentials of teamwork. Teamwork means relationships.

In his classic book *The Five Dysfunctions of a Team*, Patrick Lencioni illustrates that the process of teamwork all begins with trust, which leads to courageous and respectful debate and conflict over strategy and execution issues.[5] This leads individuals to buy in and commit, which leads to individual and mutual accountability—all of which leads to a focus on results that allows excellence. This whole process begins with quality relationships, relationships of trust. It starts with valuing people for their intrinsic worth, *a priori*. That's ERQ. ERQ realizes that to gain the world in accomplishments, possessions, and power, but to lose one's soul (a heart of love with the ability to engender love in return), is ultimate failure. And, in reality, the commitment in the heart to value relationships and the effort of the mind to understand and relate to people well leads to quality teamwork and outcomes.

Want to try it? Here are some suggestions for improving your ERQ, cultivating a relational value system, and developing a relationship investor mind-set:

- Suspend judgment and expectation. Remember that every person has a story and faces his/her own background difficulties.
- Take 100 percent responsibility for the relationship. Treat others well regardless of how they treat you or behave.
- Be more patient with people. This will increase the chances that they'll improve relationship and performance.
- View a person's immediate transgression in light of the long-term perspective of who he/she is in the bigger picture.
- Tap in to people's hearts when you give them feedback. Speak on a relational level and affirm them emotionally, which opens them up to truly listen.

This kind of value system allows you to carry your success off the field and beyond the office. It means there will still be family and friends with whom to share and enjoy your success. It *won't* allow you to puff yourself up with the false belief that you are better than others because you perform better than others. With this paradigm, you'll make it a lot easier for people to relate to you as a person—at home and at work—rather than as a taskmaster or a competitor. Such a focus will change you and usually changes relationships for the better.

Consider Your Relationship With God

Life's blitzes can open our hearts and lives to God in unprecedented ways. The crushing moments and painful chapters hold danger and opportunity from a spiritual standpoint. We can either wall off or get to know our God. Overcoming a blitz and realigning one's paradigm from a performance basis to a relational basis is a process that often opens up a dimension of life we may have ignored or marginalized.

God may not be on your radar. He may not seem real to you. If you do not believe in God, I encourage you to make this a time to reach out and test for yourself whether He exists or not. Be open to the notion of a personal, eternal, caring Creator and redeemer of fallen human experience.

Hebrew and Christian Scriptures record the Father God and God the Son saying such things as "Those who seek me find me," "Call to me," and "You will seek me and find me."[6] The key to that quest is the humility and sincerity of one's heart. And remember, everything about faith is not proven by evidence or data. That's why it's called *faith*.

If your experience fails to turn up any evidence of God, then your quest hasn't lost much of anything and you have proven your open-mindedness. On the other hand, if you *do* experience an increased sense of the reality of God and the power of faith in God, you'll have gained a relationship and dimension to life that changes everything on your journey.

If you already have a religious tradition or faith background, this is an opportunity under intense need to bring the matter of God's existence and relevance into sharp focus. Perhaps if you reach out to God in a time of challenge, you'll find something more than a religion or set of beliefs. You may find a personal manifestation of God's love for you, of God's awareness and involvement with you, of God's purpose and care for you. You may discover a more personal understanding and relationship with your Creator.

My best explanation of "turning to God" is to become *relational* toward God—whether you feel it or not. Talk within your heart or out loud, preferably alone, while walking, kneeling, driving, crying, thanking. Ask questions. *God, are you real? Will you show yourself to me? Can I know you?* Listen. Look for evidence of God. Attribute beauty and goodness and love and kindness to a Creator. Ask to see more of God. Express gratitude to God for whatever is good. Tell Him what confuses and tempts you. Hide nothing; hold nothing back. Be bold. Seek.

Ask if you can be forgiven or can forgive. Notice what you see, what happens, what messages hit you poignantly and repeatedly. Ask. Ask. Ask again. Then listen along the course of life, in all moments and situations, but especially in silence and solitude. Make the effort to pull away from the pace, the noise, and the media. Take a walk, a hike, a climb, or a drive into nature. Set aside characterizations of what the Bible says. Read it for yourself.

One caveat: Do all this with an attitude of humility. Pride will blind us and kill anything good. Humility opens the door to all good things, in a relationship with the Creator AND with your fellow human beings.

The Powerful Leverage of a Relational Value System

The ultimate success of a transcendent value system goes beyond the immediate reward of enhanced relationships, personal peace, and satisfaction. A huge bonus of the relationally based investor paradigm is the trust it builds between individuals, which allows them to accomplish dramatically more together than they could ever have accomplished solo. Trust lies at the heart of teamwork, leveraging the power of various people's strengths in a complementary and multiplying way.

As we will see in the next chapter, a relational value system *unleashes the power of team, and team is key to overcoming any blitz in life, turning pain into gain, trial into triumph, and personal loss into blessing others.*

Time Out for Self-Reflection

Review the self-questions on pages 79–80. Think about it: On what basis are you most likely to evaluate and treat people—performance, popularity, power, possessions, or positions? Be honest. Think of examples where that standard played out in your life, both in personal and work relationships. Then answer

- What might you have done differently?
- What WILL you do differently in the future?

Run the Play: Practical Application

What are some ways you can demonstrate to family, co-workers, or teammates your commitment to a relational value system, rather than a performance-based one?

Family: _____

_____

Co-workers: _____

_____

Teammates: _____

_____

Friends/Others: _____

_____

Consider your relationship with God. Pull away from the noise, invest some time to seek and examine and ask. Go to the source; read the Bible. The books Genesis and John both start with, "In the beginning . . ." Humble your heart and consider. Seek to grow closer, to know God's love.

6

Be an Investor, Not a Consumer

Consumer:

One that consumes: (1) one that utilizes economic goods; (2) an organism requiring complex organic compounds for food, which it obtains by preying on other organisms or by eating particles of organic matter.

Investor:

1. One who commits (money) in order to earn a financial return.

2. One who involves himself or engages, especially emotionally. They were deeply *invested* in their children's lives.

Usually we think of consumers and investors in terms of the economy, not relationships—or football. However, the analogy does work! Here's what it can look like in that context:

Super Bowl champion coach Mike Holmgren started in the NFL as an assistant coach under Bill Walsh. One day, Holmgren was standing next to Walsh as Jerry Rice caught a crisply thrown pass from Joe Montana in a scrimmage. The defensive coverage wasn't tight, and Rice turned the slant into a sprint up the field for a touchdown. Walsh frowned as he turned to young Holmgren,

91

who was just beginning as Montana's tutor. "That pass is not what we want. It was too close to Jerry's chest. It should have been six inches in front of his pads."

From that point forward, Holmgren coached quarterbacks to a standard of accuracy similar to those of heart surgeons or NASA engineers.

In NFL facilities around the league, quarterback coaches are teaching elite quarterbacks like Drew Brees, Aaron Rodgers, and Russell Wilson to throw the ball to receivers in a target diameter of one foot. This perfectly serves the receiver so that he need not stretch, bend, jump, or dive. It makes the catch easier, the run after the catch more effective, and the chance of a first down or touchdown for the team more likely. Quarterbacks should *serve* receivers with meticulous accuracy.

Meanwhile, in meeting rooms and throughout practices, receivers' coaches are saying this to wide receivers: "If you can touch it, you gotta catch it." Great receivers catch anything close to them. They make the quarterback and the team look good. Dive. Leap. Lay out. Take a hit, but catch the ball. *Sacrifice.*

Quarterbacks and receivers must have investor mentalities. Both groups are aiming to serve their teammates with the highest standard possible. They realize the other position is tough to play, with defenders flying all around them. They focus on the excellence they expect of themselves, not the other position.

Imagine, however, if coaches told quarterbacks to expect receivers to catch anything close, or if they told the receivers that quarterbacks should put every ball in perfect position. The expectations would switch from what *they* will do for their teammate to what their *teammate* will do for them. That's a consumer mentality. Quarterbacks would inevitably lessen their standards of delivering easy-to-catch passes, with defenders about to crush them. Receivers would start putting out less sacrificial effort to catch any pass, especially the inaccurate ones. It would kill the teamwork—and the team.

In a session for the ESPN feature *Sports Science*, Drew Brees threw ten out of ten passes into a 4.8-inch-diameter bull's-eye from twenty yards. Every pass left Drew's hand at exactly 52 mph with a 6-degree launch angle.

When asked if it were necessary to be that accurate, his answer was, "Absolutely!" He explained that receivers are covered by defenders, who leave windows of opportunity so small that the ball often needs to be in an exact spot to give the receiver and team a chance for a completion.

Brees is legendary for his practice habits, accuracy, and performance. He doesn't do it so he can win accuracy contests. He does it because he's an *investor*. He's committed to being the best so that he can serve his receivers and teammates, lifting them to their mutual peak performance.

Contrast Drew Brees's expectations of himself with those of a prima donna wide receiver, who waves his arms to show the quarterback and viewing world that "he's open." Think of the athlete who elevates himself over teammates while demanding center stage, who whines in the press about not being featured enough, or who makes excuses for not performing well.

Got it? If so, you've got the consumer attitude picture contrasted against the investor attitude.

Trained to Be a Consumer

"Have it your way."

"Our number one goal is your happiness."

"Go ahead, pamper yourself. You're worth it."

Since we were little kids, we've been hearing and assimilating the messages. According to the Media Dynamics publication *Media Matters*, a typical adult experiences potential daily exposure of about 600 to 625 ads in any form. Of these exposures, 272 come from the major traditional media such as TV, radio, magazines, and newspapers.[1]

> Ask not what your country can do for you; ask what you can do for your country.
>
> John F. Kennedy

Jeremy, a twenty-nine-year-old man describing the *zeitgeist*—spirit of the times—of this me-centered advertising age, told me this:

> I think one of the major challenges for my generation is consumerism. We have grown up in a country that has known incredible prosperity and freedom, and we have been inundated with advertisements since we were born. We are the customers, and the customers are always right. We have been taught by society not to be satisfied with what we have. We need to update and upgrade constantly or we become outdated and irrelevant. Most of us have never had to learn how to be content. Most of us would never admit to thinking like consumers, but it remains at the core of our culture and foundation of our society. It's almost impossible not to be affected by it and not let it spill over into our relationships.

Consumerism has trained us to be even more focused on ourselves than we would be on our own. A consumer has a hard time wrapping his head around considering others before himself or thinking about what he can do for others.

What Can I Get? vs. What Can I Give?

So often I'm not at all like the two generous brothers from the Jewish story earlier. Their others-centered lens is a stark contrast to the more common human experience of putting self first. One approach to life asks, "What can I *get*?" The other asks, "What can I *give*?"

This is the consumer/investor paradigm, which can be a useful analogy for identifying, understanding, and applying the difference between a performance-based and a relationally based value system. Learning to ask yourself, "Am I a consumer or an investor?" in every situation or relationship is a swift and powerful way to assess and transform your approach to life.

Use the exercise below to do a quick check on your mind-set and values. It can change the way you think, feel, act, and speak.

CONSUMERS . . .

- Go into a situation thinking, *What can I get out of this?*
- Enter conversations wanting to impress or win points.
- Want to know what others can do for them, seeking advantage for themselves.
- Want to cut in front of others in long lines or skirt around traffic, behaving aggressively to avoid having to wait like everyone else.
- Want everything to be convenient for themselves more than for others.
- Want their kids to do well and receive recognition so that they can enjoy the status and satisfaction of identifying with or taking credit for them.
- Won't apologize because it's awkward and costs them something (pride).
- Look for the fastest way to get what they want from others, even resorting to manipulation or bullying, oblivious to the fact that others may feel used.
- Justify compromise as a means to an end.
- Often engage in white lies and half-truths, all the while deceiving others.
- Withhold information and opportunities that would give an advantage to others.
- Compare people and relationships, often jealously overestimating others' happiness compared to their own.
- Intently look for the best seat in the room or car or at the table, etc.
- Want to win arguments, land a sharp retort, and be "right."
- Come home at night wanting to be served or left alone.
- Want to be understood more than to understand others.
- Dominate conversations without asking questions or listening.

- Are driven by the desire to be popular.
- Choose friends and date people for selfish reasons, ignoring the emotional vulnerabilities of others.
- Treat sex as an à la carte item in their own buffet line of life.
- Consistently take credit for team efforts.
- Put others down or withhold praise so as to build up themselves.

INVESTORS . . .

- Go into a situation thinking, *How can I bless others or add value to their lives?*
- Enter conversations with curiosity about other people, hoping to learn more about them.
- Seek to understand before seeking to be understood.
- Want to know what they can do to help others, aiming to validate and encourage them.
- Recognize others' wishes and are happy to accommodate.
- Consider the long term when it comes to relationships.
- Take joy in giving consideration to others and seeing their pleasure, practicing kindness unconditionally.
- Handle traffic with patience and are courteous toward fellow drivers, even when they're behaving rudely such as trying to cut in to gain for themselves a better position.
- Don't insist on self-convenience when it inconveniences or competes with others.
- Avoid comparing their children's achievements to others' children.
- Understand the dividends of apologizing and forgiving, rejecting bitterness.
- Avoid shortcuts, selfish requests, and manipulation.

- Won't bully, demand, or whine in their relationships.
- Stick to honesty, self-disclosure, and transparency when facing a conflict, even when it doesn't reflect well on them.
- Share information and opportunities that would give an advantage to or assist others.
- Honor the truth for the purpose of loving others.
- Minimize the faults of others, dealing honestly but with no extra portions of guilt or shame.
- Can keep a secret and protect a confidence, avoiding gossip and public criticism.
- Do their best to bring optimism and hope to people and situations, with a "glass half full" attitude and "the sun will come up tomorrow" influence.
- Seek to understand what is unique about others and what motivates them by taking a genuine interest in each of their relationships.

A consumer values people *conditionally*. An investor values people as a *priority*. When you do this, you give a great blessing to others, bringing out the best in them and in yourself. My father used to encourage us to treat people at all stations in life with importance, aware that our paths in life often cross again. He also encouraged us to be *grateful*.

One of the keys to thinking and acting like an investor is gratitude. Think about it: The more grateful you are, the more likely you are to give of yourself to others.

Psychology Today published an article titled "The Benefits of Gratitude," which mentions,

> Gratitude is an emotion expressing appreciation for what one has—as opposed to, say, a consumer-oriented emphasis on what one wants or needs. . . . Studies show that . . . grateful thinking—and especially expression of it to others—is associated with increased levels of energy, optimism, and empathy.[2]

Energy, optimism, and empathy for others are the fuel to invest in people and relationships.

On the other hand, when we're not grateful, we tend to take a short-term approach and are self-serving toward others. This not only hurts them, it damages the relationship and brings less satisfaction, and more pain, upon us. When we have a conditional, performance-based value system, we are only shooting *ourselves* in the foot! Being a consumer in relationships simply doesn't work.

What Consumers and Investors Can Look Like

Service and gratitude will fuel your relationship; entitlement and expectation will poison it.

Steve Maraboli, *Unapologetically You:
Reflections on Life and the Human Experience*

Craig hadn't wanted a divorce, but it happened anyway. He was now a recently divorced dad, still in the throes of the hurt and negativity from the breakup. His ex-wife called him one morning in a panic—awkwardly so, under the circumstances—because her car had broken down and she had nowhere else to turn. "I've got to get to work. What do I do?" she asked in desperation.

Craig could have just politely recommended a good mechanic or done even less than that. Instead, he rearranged his whole day to put her needs first. He drove over to his ex-wife's house, gave her his car, and then proceeded to get her car fixed.

Craig's daughter caught wind of what was going on. His demeanor and his willingness to put her mother first, despite the recent history between them, blew her away. She said, "Dad, how can you treat her so well when she's been treating you the way she has?"

Craig replied, "God loves us unconditionally. Jesus doesn't just call us to treat people well who also treat us well. We treat them nicely all the time. We don't just love people when they're easy to love; we love them always."

Think about the example Craig set for his daughter and for anyone else in his family. Think too about the emotional freedom in which a person like Craig lives. Freedom from the bondage of unforgiveness, bitterness, and retaliation—freedom to give, to rise above circumstances, and to invest in other people for *their* good more than one's own. It's clear that a divorced, single dad modeled love and marriage really, really well for his kids that day. He demonstrated that no blitz disqualifies us from responding with love and kindness, and to be a positive influence on people, including the most important people watching us—our kids.

Often, though, we don't control our emotions and actions as well as Craig did. We react out of a short-term, self-centered, and judgmental frame of reference. My wife and I recently experienced that sort of reaction when we found ourselves on the receiving end of a consumer-based value system, from an airline employee who was boarding us on a flight. We were in boarding group three, awaiting our turn. After all the group-two passengers had boarded, there was no one in line. I was in a bit of a consumer mode, impatient to board the plane and store our luggage. I told Stacy (the investor type who considers others before herself) we could get in line to board now that all the group twos were done. When we approached the attendant, Stacy told the person we were in group three, but since the line had thinned, we had come forward.

The airline employee responded in an uppity tone, "That's my job. *I'll* decide when the groups board," rubbing it in a bit. She then called for more group-two passengers, of which there were none, to show us who was in charge. When none came forward, she quickly announced for group three to begin boarding. At that point, she seemed more interested in being in charge than in caring for the customers in group two, much less those of us in group three.

If she'd been bringing a relationship-investor attitude to her job, she'd have said "Have a nice flight," and *then* asked if there were any other group-two passengers, to be sure she was being fair to them. Relationship investors realize that the business exists to serve the customer, not to have the customer serve and obey the company. A consumer-mentality employee, on the other hand, prefers the short-term, and fleeting, gratification of telling others off, showing who's in control, and pointing out others' failings in any given situation.

See the difference?

Investor vs. Consumer in the Workplace

Relationships are never about power, and one way to avoid the will to power is to choose to limit oneself—to serve.

Wm. Paul Young, *The Shack: Where Tragedy Confronts Eternity*

I once spoke with an entrepreneur in Florida who operates Chick-fil-A restaurants and employs about fifty people. I asked him what issues he was dealing with to create a team of excellence. He told me he fully believed in training his people in operational excellence, teamwork, and customer service. But when I mentioned the consumer/investor paradigm, his body kind of shivered, and his eyes grew wide. It was an "aha" moment for him as he remarked on how much sense that paradigm made. He could immediately imagine, from that perspective, how to behave toward his teammates and managers. He recognized how much he'd love for certain ones to gain the clarity and benefit of making the shift from a consumer mind-set to an investor mind-set.

I believe the consumer/investor paradigm is the key to building trust, teamwork, unity, commitment, and synergy—to sharing lasting partnerships and a better future together.

Here's a good exercise. Ask yourself

- In this situation, am I thinking and acting like an investor or a consumer?
- Am I considering the long-term and the mutual interests of others, or am I focused on the immediate, on my own gratification and interests?

- Am I thinking about the withdrawals I'll make from others' accounts, or am I focused on the investments I'll make in them to meet their needs now, and which lead to mutual and personal dividends in the future?
- Am I thinking about the team or about myself alone?

A football player who skips his personal weight training and conditioning efforts, who shows up late to team meetings or practices, who fails to watch game film and study his weekly game plan is a player who's making his week a bit more leisurely and comfortable, yet he's denying his teammates his fullest preparation and dependability. It will extract a cost when others are demotivated in their workouts and practices by the unequal and inadequate contribution of a teammate. Teammates may be tempted to slacken their efforts under the emotional excuse, "If he's not going to give it all and do his part, why should I sacrifice so much?" The cost and damage will show up on game day: a player's missed assignment, slow reactions due to poor preparation, or fourth-quarter fatigue due to slack conditioning—all of which will lead to trouble and failure. A player not making a block, tackle, or catch with the game on the line can cause the whole team's season to be in jeopardy, if not ruined entirely. As a result, the team misses the playoffs, players earn lower bonuses, and all are worth a bit less in the next round of contract negotiations and endorsement deals. One player's consumer attitude can rub off on others until eventually the team has lost its identity as a team of one and instead functions as a bunch of individuals and "stars."

The paradigm of consumer versus investor operates effectively for cultivating a team mentality whether in sports or work, or any other context or environment. It puts hands and feet to an aspect of teamwork that can seem too abstract. For example, if you tell someone to be "unselfish and team-oriented," that's a vague and subjective directive. It can be difficult for some people to grasp such a concept, much less apply in practical ways to their business relationships and interactions. Instead, paint the consumer/investor paradigm and show how investors add value to their teammates and organization. Urge them to ask, "Am I acting like a *consumer* or an *investor* in this situation? Am I focused on making contributions and deposits, or am I focused on what I can take or withdraw from a situation, person, or organization?"

The Power of Connection

My friend Jerry has gone through two huge blitzes in life. First, in the prime of his life he lost his wife to cancer. After five years of grief, he regained a passion to reinvent and rededicate himself to his financial services business and, with several years of planning and preparations, arranged a corporate retreat to present his grand ideas and strategy to his network of associates. Unfortunately, they didn't buy it. It all went down in flames faster than he could imagine.

He was rejected by former associates and clients. Six years to the day after the loss of his wife, he lost the business he had built up over three decades.

"It was my life's opus," Jerry shared as he recalled Richard Dreyfuss in *Mr. Holland's Opus*. He had owned a stake in a national company and had an organization with $30 million in revenue. "Losing it all was like getting hit in the jaw."

He had labored intensely, prayed like crazy, and prepared intently, but he'd missed some crucial things: His emotional and physical absence over the years after he lost his wife caused him to lose relational capital with his clients, the associates. He'd also been detached since his sale of the company into an international entity.

Yet Jerry's story turned increasingly positive with time.

A teamwork theme began to emerge after his wife's death, and even more so after the loss of his company. It wasn't initiated by Jerry, who admits to being an achiever, and a fairly isolated, self-sufficient one at that. Like many leaders, he had a huge business network but had constructed an insulated life. Then, a man who had also lost a wife reached out to console and coach Jerry. Shortly after, Jerry got remarried to a wonderful woman. Friendships grew more important, and Jerry began meeting weekly with a group of friends (of which I was one), opening up about the deep things in life.

"A crucial pathway for me through my blitz was community," Jerry declares. It became the taproot of his new life and business.

He pursued training in executive coaching and has discovered a seemingly insatiable passion for reading, learning, and the power of small groups. Today he is in his dream job, combining the life lessons from his blitzes with the joy of providing community for the personal and leadership development of business peers.

Jerry's blitzes shook him up, slowed him down, and changed him:

> A key to facing the blitz is to realize it's about perspective. When the horizontal circumstances and relationships are falling apart around you, it's time to look for and seize the vertical perspective. I could have done better, but I did focus on God, the vertical relationship.
>
> Key Scriptures helped me realize that my identity and primary relationship are in Christ. I read those key passages almost weekly, and focused on His love for me. I am secure in Him.

Jerry realized that it wasn't about his performance. "My regrets are that I thought I could do and have it all. I had two compartments back then: my Christian-beliefs compartment and my living-in-the-world, business-success compartment. That just doesn't work."

Compartmentalization is not sustainable in the long run. Our core values, spiritual perspective, faith . . . all of these should inform and shape every area of our lives and work.

Jerry describes his ultimate realization that "My life was meant to demonstrate God's greatness, not my own. I was intended to bless other people, not myself.

> My eyes were opened to my self-centeredness and selfishness. I was moving from "doing" to "being." I sensed God was whispering to

me about a new way of living . . . a more peaceful, more fulfilling, and more humble way of living. Stage One of this new way of living was to realize that it's not about me. Stage Two was more important. It's the passionate conviction that "It's all about *you*." It's about my focus on you . . . loving, serving, and uplifting you. Jesus was that way . . . fully present for and focused on the people He met and healed.

I see today that God made me an achiever, and that's fine. But the purpose of achieving has changed to seeking God's glory and the other person's development, their good.

As his friend, I've witnessed Jerry become more others-focused. He has become acutely aware of the huge need that business leaders have for friendships with other leaders who understand what they experience day-to-day, and who have the courage to tell one another what they need to hear. We all have blind spots, but Jerry likes to say that with such a small community of leaders helping one another, the blind spots melt away.

The blitz of losing his business, compounded by the grief he went through in losing his wife, has opened Jerry to a new reality of gifts that are just beginning to multiply.

As I look back on my previous career, I'd deployed my natural gifts and talents in a way that had been successful in terms of making money, with some degree of fulfillment. But upon much reflection, I see that the fulfillment came in fits and starts and was never complete. The fulfillment of investing in my passion to help leaders become successful in who they can be, not just what they can do, is almost beyond description of how cool that is for me.

This time around in business, the gifts and blessings are not so much financial as they are spiritual and relational.

Jerry's Lessons in Facing the Blitz

- **Get out of isolation, get into community.** It's important for peer leaders to speak truth to and challenge one another to face the truth. I call this "Carefrontation."

- **Grow as a leader.** As a CEO or high-level business leader, your company's growth, culture, and long-term prosperity will always be limited by your own blind spots, and can be enhanced by your leadership development.

- **Embrace Quietness.** When you find yourself in a cocoon, do not rush your way through it. This is a time where God's love shines brightest in our hearts, and where He can grow us the most.

- **Embrace the Vertical.** Seek relationship with God. Look for His bigger picture. Ask, "What is God trying to do in me?"

- **Truly, it's all about others.** Focus on love, serve and uplift others. Help others thrive and succeed.

> Life must be lived forward, but can only be understood backwards.
>
> Søren Kierkegaard

Apply It in Your Business

A relational value system—investing in people—may not seem to make a lot of sense in business, especially in today's business world. Not true. Valuing relationships is the foundation for investing in the people who make up an organization or team.

A relational value system and relational investor approach boosts morale. It develops a positive corporate culture. It inspires both employee and consumer confidence. If you've got a relational value system and people know you care about them, there's a greater degree of trust overall. Trust and valuing relationships engender greater honesty, along with honest feedback about business issues.

In his bestselling business books, teamwork guru Patrick Lencioni points out that trust leads to engaging more of the talent, intelligence, and opinions of the whole team. Because of that, the manager or business owner can make better decisions. It helps employees and managers alike engage in honest dialogue, issue-based conflict, and fierce conversations around team goals. With respected relationships, high trust, and courageous dialogue, the whole team benefits.

A relational value system in the workplace fuels investment in others. It also gives people freedom to risk—and to fail. Without freedom to fail, people won't take risks. Innovation is stifled. Without innovation, performance won't improve and people won't succeed at as high a rate than if your work environment fostered a relationally based value system.

In 1988 and 1996, I joined my dad for several of his campaigning efforts in the presidential primaries and presidential election. One of the things he consistently did that stood out to me, and especially to those who were used to how political campaigns are typically run, was to work his way through the kitchen of the hotel or restaurant where events were being held. There, he asked names and questions, praised the food, chatted about football, and generally made the cooks and waitstaff feel great. More so than telling me, I remember him showing me that we should treat everyone in a special way and assure them they're important to us. "You never know when you'll run into them again," he'd say. Build bridges, not regrets. Do what you can, in ways that aren't predictable, to let your people know they're noticed, valued, and important.

A relational value system builds trust, increases innovation, and encourages the furthering of team interaction and the accomplishment of team goals. This approach honors each team member's uniqueness and perspective. They'll try harder, and better decisions will arise. Relationships help results!

No Regrets

Another advantage of a relationally based and investor-oriented value system is that it's one of the best ways to prevent a lifetime of regrets. Most seniors, when polled about their biggest regrets in life, don't tend to cite regrets like wishing they had achieved, accumulated, or accomplished more. Rather, across the board, they regret things that would have benefited them relationally had they paid more attention to them earlier:[3]

1. I didn't spend enough time with my loved ones.
2. I didn't tell my family and friends that I loved them often enough.
3. I was too stubborn or proud to admit my mistakes and apologize.
4. I chose bitterness over reconciliation.
5. I allowed my life to be consumed by work.
6. I was too hesitant to take risks and try new things.
7. I wasted too much time.
8. I didn't appreciate the little things in life.
9. I valued things over relationships.
10. I worried too much.

Dennis Trittin, life and financial literacy expert and author of the book *What I Wish I Knew at 18*, recommends doing a periodic self-evaluation. Do any of these regrets apply to you? Be honest! If they do, then do something about it.

A relational value system helps prevent regrets and the burning of relational bridges. An investor approach adds value to people and relationships, deepening our character and bettering our future. Most people realize later in life that you may need to circle back and cross some rivers more than once, and when you do, you find it was wise not to have burned that bridge!

Time Out for Self-Reflection

Review the list of consumer and investor traits at the start of this chapter. Think and pray about who you want to be, how you want to change, and the people you want to invest in.

Run the Play: Practical Application

Copy or adapt these questions for your own use, then make them available as a daily reminder. Post them on your cell phone, the home screen of your computer or tablet, or perhaps your refrigerator:

- In this situation, am I thinking and acting like an investor or a consumer?
- Am I considering the long term and the mutual interests of others, or am I focused on the immediate, on my own gratification and interests?
- Am I thinking about the withdrawals I'll make from others' accounts, or am I focused on the investments I'll make in them to meet their needs now and which lead to mutual and personal dividends in the future?
- Am I thinking about the team or about myself alone?

Reach Out to Others

7

Look to the Team Around You

People who work together will win, whether it be against complex football defenses or the problems of modern society.

Vince Lombardi

In 1986, I was traded away from the Rams and showed up in San Francisco as a new backup to Joe Montana, the future Hall of Fame quarterback. After a physical and mental hurricane of preparation to learn a new offense, I settled into the regular season, mostly to support Joe and our team from the sidelines. In a surprise turn of events, however, Joe was injured during our first game of the year in Tampa. A subsequent back surgery the following week threatened Joe's and, as some skeptics warned, the 49ers' entire season. Suddenly, the team's fortunes were in the hands of a barely trained new quarterback in Bill Walsh's dynamic West Coast offense.

How was that going to work? A lot of people wondered. But I didn't have any time to waste with wondering.

The intensity of the situation had my adrenaline surging during that entire first week, and it peaked during pregame warm-ups of the game versus the LA Rams—the team that had just traded me to San Francisco. All-Pro receiver Dwight Clark ribbed me later for how hard I threw the ball just playing catch on the sidelines before that game. Even though Dwight had gloves on, he called a younger receiver over to catch for me in his place, complaining that I was hurting his hands!

For the 49ers (and me) to successfully replace Joe was going to require the fullest measure of my study and practice, and a heroic dose of teamwork. Coaches tutored me, players stepped up, and I did fine. Things turned out well, and in the six weeks I played, the team's offense operated well together and my quarterback rating rose to the top of the league. Then, when I was injured after six games, Mike Moroski stepped in to quarterback the next two games. Montana was out for half the season, but we all pulled together to help our team stay in contention for when he returned. Weeks later, we won our division and went on to the playoffs, despite the blitz of injuries to our team's quarterbacks.

> A burden shared is half the burden. A joy shared is twice the joy.
>
> Anonymous

Facing blitzes isn't done alone. It requires *teamwork*. Unless we see through the lens of team relationships and draw upon the power of people helping one another, we'll be handicapped in facing life's blitzes. We'll likely miss the silver linings and the valuable pearls that come from facing a blitz together. Life is made better by teamwork, in many ways. Yet it's far from easy or automatic.

Better Together

People were made for teamwork. I would go so far as to say that humans were *designed* for teamwork—for creative, interdependent relationships with other people. In the biblical account of creation, one of the first things the Creator says about human beings is, "It is not good for the man to be alone."[1]

The human body itself is a remarkable picture of teamwork and synergy. Two legs enable us to run. Arms contribute counter-synchronized pumping. Our brain calibrates balance and the firing of muscles. Our eyes and ears provide a read on the terrain. Everything we do is a combination of all our different body parts working together. If one part is wounded, diseased, or ceases to function, the whole body suffers.

Unfortunately, not everyone sees life—and teamwork—in that context. Humans are so gifted and talented, and we Westerners in particular live in a prosperous and consumer-driven society. All too often we fool ourselves by thinking we are (or should be) independent and self-sufficient. This mind-set hurts us in several ways:

> Coming together is a beginning; keeping together is progress; working together is success.
>
> Henry Ford

1. It shrinks our capacity for what we can accomplish. We can ultimately achieve more in unity than in isolation. We're better together than alone.

2. It leaves us with a sense of emptiness or loneliness. Alone, we are unable to share our experiences of difficulty or success with others.

3. It misses the human reality that our default condition and weakness is selfishness. Teamwork and commitment challenge our selfishness and cause us to become less proud, more humble, and easier to get along with—more pleasant, generous, and happy.

As the 2008 NBA season began, history's most prolific championship team was twenty years into a drought of no NBA titles. Boston Celtics coach Doc Rivers was faced with a good news/bad news dilemma. He had three über-talented basketball players who each had been a superstar in his own right on a previous team: Ray

Allen, Paul Pierce, and Kevin Garnett. Normally a scenario like that would not be a formula for great teamwork, with (potentially) big egos and highly individualized playing styles.

But Coach Rivers wanted unity, and he had a trick up his sleeve. Actually, it was a word. *Ubuntu.*

> He who wants to go fast, travels alone. He who wants to go far, travels together.
>
> N'gambai African Proverb

Ubuntu is a Zulu word meaning, "I am because we are." Rivers unpacked the word and the vision for a team-first identity. *Ubuntu* developed into a chant the whole team used as they broke every huddle at practices and games en route to their first NBA championship in twenty-two years. That season, all the players—including stars Allen, Pierce, and Garnett—submitted themselves to a larger identity and cause: the team. Teamwork dominated, not egos. Players sacrificed and assisted for each other. They thrived.

My wife and I are a team. We too experience and benefit from *ubuntu*. The well-being of our marriage (the whole) matters to the two of us (the individuals). Our identities are wrapped up in our relationship and unity as one. Our marriage matters to other people, and theirs matters to us. Our children matter to each other at a deeper level because we are a family.

American initiative and values have great merit, but not when we take our individualism too far. When we insist on our individual rights and interests, independent of other people, we end up hurting others, we erode relationships, and we hurt ourselves. You matter to me, as a fellow human, another unique and valuable child of God. Ultimately my identity, purpose, and happiness are joined to yours. We are at our best when we are a community rather than when we stand alone. We've got to learn to think like a team. *Ubuntu!* How do you build it? It doesn't start with the mechanics; it starts with the mind-set. You start with building a teamwork *mentality*—an identity connected to others. This is the starting point for the relationships and trust required to thrive in the teamwork of life, whether at home, in sports, or at work.

Building Teams Through Trust and Managed Conflict

In *The Five Dysfunctions of a Team*, Patrick Lencioni identifies five dysfunctions that contribute to the lack of a teamwork mentality in an organization:[2]

It's interesting that trust—or the lack of trust—is the foundational block on Lencioni's pyramid. I couldn't agree more strongly. From my own experiences—in football, family, or business—I've observed that without trust, you have no team and NO CAPACITY for building one.

To review the purpose of a team, **a team exists to achieve results.** Lencioni's principles are helpful in using the challenges facing your team to actually BUILD the team in the face of a blitz rather than tear it apart. Review the pyramid illustration above and observe the five levels:

1. **Trust.** We must be honest about who we are, what we're facing, and what we're thinking (vulnerability).

2. **Proactive Engagement in Conflict.** We must have a productive, issue-centered, frank debate surrounding matters important to team results.
3. **Achieving Commitment.** Success doesn't depend on unanimity or even consensus. *Buy-in* is what counts. This occurs after all voices have been heard. Then commitment and clarity are followed by "cascading communication"—telling next layer teammates by voice within twenty-four hours.
4. **Embracing Accountability.** An honest and transparent leader sets the tone by confronting behaviors, so that peers will hold each other accountable to keeping their commitments.
5. **Focusing on Results.** Effective leaders focus everyone on the largest, most-in-common team results *first*, as the context for their personal results (which cumulatively produce the large team result).

Meetings and conference calls would be way more effective and tolerable if they had some of what NFL huddles have—high stakes and intensity. They need more than an agenda; they need a vital issue that is not yet solved or maximized. It can be a team-alignment or results issue that deserves debate, different outlooks, and opposing opinions in order to find the best solution.

Generally, team members tend to be so distant that, when together, they seek a false harmony more than they seek debate about the decisions that must be made and problems that must be fixed. Tapping the strengths of teammates and forging the alignment necessary for great teamwork result from honest, spirited debate, not bland report giving.

Here's the paradigm: The best teamwork results from an investment mentality, rather than a consumer mentality. An investor identifies with the team, the whole. They give rather than take. Candidly, it's a risk that doesn't guarantee better circumstances every time. But it does create better character and relationship integrity. Those traits equip people and teams to best respond to blitzes and challenging circumstances.

NFL football often offers us both extremes on the spectrum of teamwork. Not long ago, I saw one league franchise publicly demonstrate a most extreme version of underachieving, a team with a self-proclaimed defensive genius as head coach and with talent as deep as any team in the league. They tanked down the stretch that year and even experienced a twenty-eight-player brawl at a practice, despite desperate chastising from their coach who called them "undisciplined."

What's going on with this team? I'm thinking it traces back to a collection of individual attention-gatherers, led by a coach who probably sets that tone. When people are pushing for their own personal franchise, it's inevitable that trust goes AWOL.

Life Lessons From the Locker Room

As you may have already noticed, I've found that much of what we need to know about life, leadership, and teams can be learned in the locker room. Yes—the locker room! That's where you'll find a diverse group of guys who didn't choose to be together. They come from varying backgrounds and races, with different talents and motivations. Talk about a ripe environment for a total lack of trust! However, their mutual success is fully dependent upon building enough trust and teamwork to combine their talents, differences, and strengths. They have to learn to compensate for their respective weaknesses so that they can align, coordinate, train, sacrifice, improve, improve, improve—and win! Then they keep on working together to overcome losses and injuries in order to *keep on winning.*

Look back again to the first step in this journey that leads to VICTORY. It's building *trust*, as Lencioni identified in his pyramid diagram. And from my experience—a lesson from the locker room, if you will—it's the selfless guys who are the ones you trust the most. They're the ones you can count on in a crisis or turn to as a friend in your time of need. These guys have character, the basis of trust.

When a five-foot-eleven receiver with below average speed goes from being a low-round draft pick to the Hall of Fame, there must be some special characteristics about him. Steve Largent is that guy. He did as much for his team and the Seattle Seahawks franchise as any player in the NFL. Steve's drive to excellence was unmatched, but it was his humility that carried others along. He was a superstar who deflected praise to his team, blocked with zeal, and played special teams when needed.

At the start of training camp each year for the several seasons we played together, Steve led an effort to personally welcome all the rookies and winsomely invite them to be part of a player-led Bible study and prayer group. Steve's contagious passion for the game AND for the players kept the Seahawks alive during the team's early years as a new franchise, and his dependability in the clutch raised the level of play for all of us. A star who is humble, who serves and helps others, is still only a dim reflection of the example Jesus set for us. His life and mission to sacrifice himself declared the same thing He said, that He "did not come to be served, but to serve."[3]

Unity doesn't come from similarity or pep talks. It comes from identifying with others, having common purpose and dedication, being side by side, and observing each other's sacrifice and dedication to the cause. Bottom line: It's commitment to a cause over personal credit, and others over oneself, that *wins more games.* It's the power of a team that trusts.

Building Trust

Building trust isn't as easy as it sounds. Where do you start? It begins with a desire to have the kind of character others will trust and a commitment to being trustworthy.

Most of us find our biggest flaws are due to deep-seated fears and insecurities. We make compromises, take shortcuts, or slight other people because we fear we won't get our way or have our deepest needs met. The irony is that those very behaviors are the ones that ultimately compromise our relationships with other people, which is exactly why we don't get our way and our needs fail to get met. That's why the starting point for trust is to face our insecurity and aim to build relationships where we don't need to pretend or pose, where we can be accepted for who we are. The key to that is being known, which is something we all yearn for but often fear.

You can start by telling your story, in humility. Be authentic and as vulnerable as you can muster. When you tell your story, you become real to other people. At the same time you personally experience validation in your authenticity. You discover, "Wow, that may have been hard at first, but it felt good," which makes you increasingly more comfortable being real. Good-hearted people respect you for being real, especially when you reveal your hidden wounds and weaknesses. We all have them. People can trust people who are being real. Building trust builds team.

Another way to build trust is by accepting responsibility, admitting where you fall short and let others down. Make every effort to always be the *initiator* of apology, not waiting or parsing out who has more responsibility before you finally own up to yours. When those around you see your authenticity, vulnerability, and humility in this area, they will increasingly trust you. Many people fear and avoid this. Hiding, avoiding, or defending erodes team, whereas taking responsibility and apologizing builds team.

Finally, a large part of teamwork is appreciating the value of other people. When we start to trust one another, we grow in the sense that we deepen our identity and meaning in relationship to the larger group. A healthy confidence in our strengths, and honesty about our weaknesses, helps us to find where we fit in our cooperative effort as a team.

It's not about me.

It's not about you.

It's about us as a team.

We are better together—a better me, a better you, a better world.

No Selfish Competition

I am a member of the team, and I rely on the team, I defer to it and sacrifice for it, because the team, not the individual, is the ultimate champion.

Mia Hamm

True and lasting teams—teams that build a legacy—seek their success and joy in the good of the whole. They live by the motto "A rising tide lifts all boats." They're comprised of individuals who invest in their teammates and their team's goals, rather than consuming from the team what they can gain for self. In an age obsessed with garnering attention, fame, and celebrity, wise people still hold to the maxim that "Much can be accomplished when there's no concern for who gets the credit." My dad saw this quote on a little sign Ronald Reagan had displayed on his desk in the Oval Office. Before him, President Harry Truman and legendary UCLA coach John Wooden were known to preach this powerful proverb.

Bill Belichick, winner of five Super Bowls (two as the defensive coordinator of the New York Giants, and three as the head coach of the New England Patriots) built this team-first environment into the Patriots. Numerous "stars" followed the coaches' lead and bought in to the personally understated and team-elevated philosophy. Tom Brady grew to be one of football's greatest champions (and celebrities) while diligently de-emphasizing himself and elevating his teammates. Formerly iconic self-promoting superstars like Randy Moss saw the fruit of this and gave up their old ways to join the more humble, team-first "Patriot Way."

It takes vision and courage to be the initiator, to be vulnerable and put the interests of others ahead of self. But it's worth it. Soon that vulnerability will be reciprocated and become the stepping-stone toward developing a strong team identity.

Teamwork Doesn't Just Happen

Teamwork doesn't happen by chance or even osmosis. It often comes as a result of a visionary person stepping up and painting a picture for the individuals as to *why* it makes sense to collaborate and sacrifice on behalf of the group. This kind of leader is able to cast the vision for the group of *how* we are better together, and *what* we can do to support each other's strengths and compensate for any weaknesses. Everything builds from a great purpose, a noble cause. Why are we together? What will we be? How will we do it?

Why.

What.

How.

The leader finds a way to help people on the team identify that they all need each other. They all have strengths and weaknesses, and by being honest about them, they can combine strengths with other people's strengths and fill in the gaps their weaknesses create. Doing so actually multiplies the value of the strengths by aligning team members strategically with others.

This requires a great deal of honesty and humility. This may sound counterintuitive. "Why be humble?" some may ask. "Humility doesn't get you ahead in life." I disagree. Sure, it's no shortcut to beating other people, if that's what is meant by *getting ahead*. But humility holds the power to heal, as we saw in chapter 2. It's been effective for the Patriots, Celtics, Coach Wooden's teams, and many other champions. That's the counterintuitive part. *Humility is actually a key to greatness.* The trick these days is that so much fame, cash, and adulation come with championships and success that humility tends to vanish, and the championships don't repeat. It's hard for people with lucrative business and high-profile careers to stay humble after the accolades and rewards have been flowing their way for a while.

Humble teammates appreciate the contributions of others and are able to highlight others' strengths. They're honest about their own strengths and don't have to pretend to be strong in ways they're not. They don't need to promote themselves, but rather choose to be their best and serve others for the mutual benefit of the team.

Without pride? What?!

That's right. No pride . . . of a certain sort, that is.

Now, you may think of pride as a good thing: pride in your school, pride in your work, pride in your country, pride in your team, pride in your value and dignity as a person.

And if that's what you mean when you talk about pride, that's great.

But the pride we need to do away with in order to cultivate a team mentality is *arrogance*. When I hurt my wife's feelings and minimize my actions or defend myself, that's bad pride. When I jockey to be treated better than others or get the credit, that's bad pride. Bad pride messes up relationships, trust, and teamwork. It affects long-term results.

So there's good pride and bad pride. Bad pride is based in arrogance, self-elevation, and independence from others. Sometimes it may appear unassuming and modest in public, but it's actually an unhealthy private attitude that you can't show weakness or need. It's a form of pride that prevents many of us from admitting we can't make it on our own, that we need others and we need help. To cite an extreme case, I had a friend who died because he would not ask for and accept the help he needed to escape alcoholism.

Good pride is based in identification with others—i.e., interdependence. This pride of attachment is different from arrogance. It's not thinking you're better than others because of your association, but rather is deeply appreciating and affirming of the group to which you are loyal. *Ubuntu* . . . I am because we are.

You can have pride in your country because of its virtues and therefore be a loyal and contributing citizen. You can have pride in your team because of the depth of your bond and sacrifice to achieve more together than alone. You can have pride in your company because you excel at serving people, and pride in a job well done because excellence matters to you more than convenience or popularity.

Bad pride, on the other hand, is quite the opposite. Arrogance is a virus that begins the decay of the immune system of our personal character. It's the initial domino that begins to knock down a succession of character compromises and dishonorable actions that hurt others, erode our integrity, and destroy the relational harmony in our lives. And arrogance is contagious. Displays of pride and credit taking can cause others on the team to become arrogant and self-focused too.

We don't often notice our arrogance and pride right away; in fact, we may not ever notice it unless we're intentional about looking for it. And if we do notice it, it doesn't always look all that bad. Sometimes arrogance will not immediately impede, but may seem to *quicken* our material advancement in the fickle marketplace of money, power, and popularity. Look more closely at those who have followed this path to its end. The corresponding bankruptcy of relational health is obvious in the lives of the rich and famous disasters of Wall Street and Hollywood. It's been the root of disgraced dictators and politicians down through history. Arrogance doesn't play out well in the long term. Many athletes have proven that. As the TV commercial warns, *Don't be that guy.*

Creating an Environment for Teamwork

Creating a positive workplace is fundamentally about teamwork. The Gallup organization interviewed 80,000 managers in 400 companies and found that great teamwork in a work environment comes from doing certain things:

- Making people feel they matter.
- Providing clarity, alignment, and relationship.
- Showing care, encouragement, and affirmation.
- Empowering them to contribute and grow.

Gallup came up with the following "12 Questions" to help business leaders measure the strength of their workplaces or teams:[4]

1. Do I know what's expected of me at work?
2. Do I have the materials and equipment I need to do my work well?
3. At work, do I have the opportunity to do what I do best every day?
4. In the last week, have I received recognition or praise for doing good work?
5. Does my supervisor, or someone at work, seem to care about me as a person?
6. Is there someone at work who encourages my development?
7. At work, do my opinions seem to count?
8. Does the mission/purpose of my company make me feel my job is important?
9. Are my co-workers committed to doing quality work?
10. Do I have a best friend at work?
11. In the last six months, has someone at work talked to me about my progress?
12. Over the last year, have I had opportunities at work to learn and grow?

My Seahawks coach, Chuck Knox, used to note outbursts of individualism and complaining on the team and then remind us, "Winning creates the environment in which all good things happen." He was a realist. He knew human nature, that we all tend to look out for number one, ourselves. He knew every player was looking at a short and risky career trajectory. Contracts were constantly up for renegotiation, and the pay would not be earned unless players made the team each year. Questioning and treatment from the media were far more tolerable when winning than losing.

And Chuck knew full well that coaches were regularly and swiftly fired when teams lose.

By reminding us about the importance of winning, Chuck was reminding us to be investors, not consumers. Focus on the team and your role, not on yourself, not on your statistics, or your salary, bonus, and contract situation, or your treatment in the press. When we all put the team first—whether in football, family, or business—we ALL increase our likelihood of winning. That's when the things you'd like to experience become far more likely and possible, and the things that hold you back, the impediments to teamwork, fade from the picture.

Bill Walsh's Keys to Teamwork

> *Blocking is the greatest act of love.*
>
> Jimmy Kemp, youth football coach;
> ex-CFL quarterback; my little brother

Teamwork doesn't come naturally or easy. We tend to be self-centered creatures. And arrogance only inflates one's view of *self*. It leads to self-seeking and short-term thinking, which undercuts the sacrifice and investment mentality that can defer gratification to create a better future. It leads to self-dependence. Arrogance leads to the "fundamental attribution error"[5]—attributing others' negative behaviors to internal character (their motives), but attributing our own negative behaviors to external environment (our circumstances). In other words, if the other guy is rude, it's because he's a rotten person. If I'm rude, it's because I'm having a bad day. Get it?

We've got to learn to see each other (and ourselves) objectively and humbly, and learn to work together. Bill Walsh used to teach us that effective teams need

1. **A compelling and uniting vision.** It's about a cause greater than any one of our individual selves, one that can only be

accomplished together. *"We know what we stand for and how we're going to do it in excellence."* Remember what Helen Keller said: The only thing worse than being blind is having sight but no vision. Vision is a picture of the future we are creating and moving toward.

2. **Appreciation and respect for the differing strengths and roles of one another.** All team members know everyone on the team well. Knowing teammates' strengths and appreciating their roles promotes a willingness to trust in each other. Once you've built that kind of trust, people are willing to commit with sacrifice.

3. **Dedication and sacrifice.** People normally don't sacrifice when they doubt it will be worth the risk and effort. But when they see it as worthwhile and trust those around them, those sacrifices are going to add up to real results. Nothing comes without dedication and sacrifice. A great team is made by dedicated people making many sacrifices. President John F. Kennedy declared an American vision to go to the moon within a decade. His vision inspired and galvanized, but he couldn't make it happen. We needed the American people's finances appropriated by Congress. We needed the talent, engineering, and technology of NASA and aeronautical companies. Finally, we needed the sacrifices of training and courageous risk-taking by the astronauts.

> Here's the question: Will you and I be the mature ones who take the risk of being consistently generous toward others, of putting others and team first?

Teamwork comes from maturity. Maturity is a combination of both consideration and courage. It's the ability to avoid "I win/you lose," or to settle for "I lose/you win." Instead it seeks a "You win/I win," because the equation starts with others, not self. It is generosity, not selfishness. A contest of generosity is a paradox, isn't it? Neither person participating loses. *This* is the culture we want to create, the teamwork we aim for, the love we dream of!

Why We All Need a Team

Does everyone have a team? Does everyone *need* to have a team? I say yes to both questions. We all need the power of team, especially in the blitzes we encounter in life.

My friend Don Wallis was a Navy fighter pilot and one of the mentors I invited along on my son Kolby's "welcome to manhood" trip, a weekend where I invited a group of friends and mentors to come together and share life stories about manhood with my eighteen-year-old son. Don shared with Kolby and six more of us men how important it is—life or death, sometimes—to operate in *team*.

Don related how he and the Navy pilots with whom he worked were trained to handle in-flight emergencies of all kinds. Among these was losing cockpit pressurization. He explained how this emergency is both subtle and dangerous. Subtle, because you have no idea the loss of pressurization has occurred; dangerous, because if you are without oxygen, you will painlessly fall asleep, never to awaken. At 40,000 feet, you would in all likelihood last no longer than sixty to seventy seconds before blackout. There is no problem if you have your oxygen mask on, however, and wearing it is a mandatory procedure.

Don swallowed all of us in his story about a training flight when he lost pressurization at 38,000 feet just before engaging his instructor in a mock dogfight. They were both flying a single-seat jet fighter; there is no one looking over your shoulder in these to keep you accountable. Don had previously unsnapped one side of his oxygen mask, and it hung loosely under his helmet. To not have your oxygen on is a combination of carelessness and overconfidence . . . perhaps arrogance as well. The jet's loss of pressure was quickly causing Don to lose his ability to think clearly; he began experiencing oxygen deprivation—hypoxic hypoxia—and was ten to fifteen seconds from blacking out. Don's flight instructor was in a jet a mile away and noticed Don slurring his words in the radio communications. He barked into Don's radio headset, "Don, put on your oxygen mask—NOW!" The command had to be repeated three times before Don could muster the act of his will to snap his mask back into place.

The quick thinking of his instructor saved Don's life. Just before blacking out, Don did as the instructor commanded. Don followed his story with this message for Kolby and each of us men: "When you're at risk because of human character flaws, be it pride, jealousy, selfishness, greed, or lust, but most particularly pride, you're usually the last one to see it. It's especially important that you build relationships with people to whom you've given permission to speak the truth to you. And when they speak into your life, LISTEN!"

We are safer when we operate in *team*—when we allow good-willed people to be close to us, when we're vulnerable and transparent with them. Like Don's superior officer, they "have our backs." They see our blind spots. Like a strong left tackle in football, they protect our "blind side." If we remain willing to hear, and they are willing to speak deeply into our lives, we'll be greatly protected and greatly blessed in every arena of life.

Great Teamwork Takes a Global Perspective

A call from Coach John Robinson in the spring of 1986 broke some interesting news to me. Knowing I'd been disappointed at getting moved from a starting role on the Rams in 1984 to the backup role in '85, he told me they'd found a "great opportunity" for me and were trading me to the San Francisco 49ers. I had assumed I'd always be on one team, so was caught off guard by the news.

As I immediately relayed the news to Stacy in our kitchen, it dawned on me that the "great opportunity" would be on a team with a well-established quarterback: Pro Bowl and Super Bowl champion Joe Montana.

I'll be stuck behind him forever, I thought as the news and situation started to sink in. Being a backup for another team, a team with the best quarterback in the league, was my great opportunity?

Looking back on it now, I can appreciate my dad's mantra: "You're in your right place." It did in fact turn out to be a great opportunity and experience. I went to one of the very best franchises in pro sports. I would be there during a heyday of excellence under Head Coach Bill Walsh, who was the best teacher and team crafter I've ever encountered. His macro to micro approach to team building was positively genius. I was taught and tested and challenged, experiencing teamwork and quarterbacking at the highest level of my career, even though it was only for part of one season!

NFL teams are large operations, made up of players with very different personalities, skills, and styles of play. They spend most of their prep time in separate meetings divided by position. Coach Walsh, however, frequently gathered the whole team to be sure that the big vision, the clear goal, was communicated to all in the context of our need for one another, and pride in our unity as a team.

When I was in Philadelphia, team-wide meetings were less common and less emphasized. John Robinson with the Rams was a master of motivation, using military history and stories, a deft sense of timing, and a keen sense of which players to call on for additional humor (usually a universally loved character nicknamed "Herc," Dennis Harrah). Walsh, however, was the coach who most inspired and elevated me through his teaching and vision-casting efforts.

One of his great keys was the knack and discipline of bringing the long-term goal and largest vision to bear upon the importance and specificity of the smallest details. Bill's philosophy was integrated and comprehensive. He didn't leave out the big picture or the detail; he would teach a play in a global manner, which has always stuck with me as a brilliant approach.

During training camp, we would be in the large team-meeting amphitheater. Most teams had position coaches install their plays in separate meetings rooms to each of the various position players. Not Bill. Before splitting up like that, Bill Walsh had all the offensive players together. Say he was installing a play-action pass like "Brown Right—Fox 2—Z Post." He'd first remind us that the play, the work we'd do on the practice field later that day, and the way we were improving from day to day and week to week were all tied to a definitive purpose—to win the Super Bowl, and to win it multiple times. To do this, we had to execute with precision and make many individual sacrifices throughout the season and on this particular play.

Bill would describe the essence of a play-action pass, predicated on the excellence of the fake run. Fooling the defense was predicated on the success of the similar-looking running plays that would precede the pass. Everything was tied to the commitment and execution that preceded it.

Next, Bill would connect the big-picture goal of the Super Bowl to the smaller picture of individual player assignments and techniques. The exact angle of steps and timing down to fractions of a second mattered. He'd teach each player's specific assignment, role, and sacrifices, relating the unique importance to each of the other positions. Bill emphasized the details of executing plays as close to perfection as possible under conditions of huge variability and opposition.

The genius of this approach was that it helped each player gain a specific and greater appreciation for the roles and sacrifices players at each position needed to make to execute the play successfully. The sacrifice by the offensive linemen of diving to their left on a "cut" block would often involve getting kneed, pounded in the helmet, or having their hands stepped on while on the ground. A running back carrying out a play-action fake with both hands wrapped around an imaginary football could be called to dive up and over the line of scrimmage, exposing himself to getting hit in the head by linebackers who assumed he had the ball. Quarterbacks had to be prepared to carry out their fake and set up to pass in less than two and a half seconds, often to be hit to the ground immediately after releasing the pass by the unblocked defensive end on the blind side.

Understanding the unique role and sacrifice of teammates at other positions gives every player a greater sense of purpose. It builds confidence in the value of doing his part, making his sacrifice, and making the play succeed. In football, unless every player acts out his role, does his job, and follows through for his teammates, there will be no success for everyone to share.

If we want to improve as contributing teammates, we need to grow. If we want to grow, we need to invest, not consume. If we want to change, then this investor/consumer paradigm in our mind and heart is a crucial and transformative approach to life. It's like a compass showing us true north so that we can navigate the tests and trials, the good and the great, the frustrations and temptations of life.

Being an investor and a team player costs something, but the highest price also generally garners the most satisfying return, especially in the face of the blitz. I've seen the investor approach create blessings and results far better than the consumer approach. I've experienced it, and I would guess that you have as well.

Time Out for Self-Reflection

1. What is your first reaction in a crisis or a challenge—to strike out on your own (independence), or to look to the team around you (interdependence)?

2. What are the teams God has placed around you in your life right now? Think about your home, extended family, neighborhood, faith community, and workplace. In what ways can you be more interdependent in your teams? How can you offer them your strengths, and draw on theirs, so that you are "better together"?

3. Do you have a mentor? Who are the most credible, caring, and wise persons you could ask to guide you through life and its blitzes?

Run the Play: Practical Application

Try This at Work or Home

1. At your conference table, dinner table, or high-stooled coffee bar, try going around the table and have each person articulate what their greatest strength is and that of the others. Identify a character-based strength and a performance-based strength. What do *you* bring to the team? Encourage others at the table to comment, affirm, or add what they see.

2. As a family, group, or team, identify a challenge or goal you're currently facing or will face in the near future. Discuss how each team member's strengths can contribute toward achieving the goal, based on their characteristics and unique contributions to the team.

3. Write down the names of people who could mentor you in family, work, career, faith, and facing a blitz. Contact them and have a conversation about mentoring.

8

Leverage the Power of LIFT

A rising tide lifts all boats.
John F. Kennedy

A candle loses nothing by lighting another candle.
Erin Majors

n the NFL, Saturday nights are when most teams sit down for meetings to go over final preparations and thoughts for the next day's game. Many watch a bit of film of the opposing team to be refreshed on how to attack their weaknesses and be aware of their strengths. But our coach at San Francisco added a different twist.

Bill Walsh had a technique I absolutely loved and saw as genius. He was the first coach I'd ever had who showed highlights of our *own* team from the prior week's game—so long as we'd won or competed admirably. He showed clips of our team in our best moments, executing plays and defending against outstanding offenses. He'd show a running play in which a running back had scored or gained big yardage. In his professorial tone, Bill would narrate the play to our team, pointing out not the obvious great run, but the amazing block by the pulling guard. He would say things that every one of us would like to hear about ourselves and were proud to hear said of our teammates.

He would say something like, "Gentlemen, take a look at our left guard Guy McIntyre on this play. Watch his footwork and speed pulling across formation and laying out to get his head in front of that linebacker he blocks. This is perfection—a great effort by a great San Francisco 49er. This is the way we play. I look forward to seeing you men play at this level tomorrow."

How do you think Guy felt when he heard that? How do you think his buddies on the team felt? How much would *you* want to be the guy to make the plays that made the highlight film the next week?

Bill used this technique to lift our sense of confidence and identity. His goal was to get us focused on our team, following through with preparation, precision, and execution. By calling out our names and highlighting us as examples of excellence, he caused us to want even more to make the sacrifices necessary to be champions. Because of this, we played with confidence in our teammates and in our coaches.

Bill wasn't perfect, but he was exceptional. He was very collegial and personal with his players, though he still commanded respect. His dry humor could cut like a scalpel, but it could also lighten the mood and loosen the team, adding a measure of fun to the relentless quest for football excellence. Most of all, Bill had a way of *lifting* our view of ourselves from average to elite, from athlete to intellectual, from winner to champion.

This is the kind of leadership I aspire to, and you can too—with your employees and teammates, your children and friends, or with anyone in your sphere of influence.

Truly Great Leadership

LIFT. If I could encapsulate the dramatic influence of truly great leadership in one word, that would be it. It's the overarching vision for this book.

My father always gave me the vision that any situation can be improved. Any problem can be overcome. Any goal can be accomplished. Any blitz can be beaten. Any trial can bring deeper meaning or growth. We can change. That's LIFT—"Life Is For Transformation."

On the last night I spent with my dad, before he passed away, I read a favorite passage of his from the Bible (Psalm 16). I prayed for him as I had done during my visits as he battled cancer. But that night I did something different, something we might not normally ask of a cancer-stricken man, weakened beyond measure. I asked Dad to pray for me, like the blessings Jewish fathers and patriarchs down through the ages have prayed for their children. Dad was so weak and tired that his words were few, but I will never forget them. He prayed, "Dear God, please help Jeff realize his talent. Help him realize the force for good [he can be in this world]. And help us both to remember the only thing that matters is 'Thy will be done.'"

Even in his deepest pain, his toughest blitz, his final moments, he prayed for me. Dad affirmed my identity by calling out my strengths and tying them to a vision for my life. It was in his DNA to encourage, to affirm, to *lift*. In fact, if there's a single word to remember him by, and a single description of the mission I want to exemplify in my life, it's LIFT!

My dad was the ultimate encourager. He told his children repeatedly, "You're in your right place. Your day will come. I love you. I am so proud of you." It was my dad who planted that same vision, optimism, and persevering confidence in me. He once watched a game of mine and told me I looked great.

"Dad," I said, "I didn't even get in the game."

"I know," he said. "You looked great throwing in warm-ups before the game and on the sideline!"

He always saw in us our best potential. He pointed out the positive and empowered us with that vision for our best. The greatest lesson to draw from his life, I believe, is the idea of LIFT. Always do what you can to lift other people to their highest and best; whether it's your team, your family, your company, or the discouraged, excluded, or oppressed. Do what you can do to lift their sights, their confidence, and their performance. Put wind beneath other people's wings. Lift the outlook, the discussion, or the debate to a higher level.

I shared at his funeral these words of LIFT that I believe he would share with every one of us in this great nation:

> All of your life has been but a preparation for this day and what you will do from this day forward. You are all God's children. You go nowhere by accident. Become what you were meant to be and spread opportunity so that others can reach their dream and be what they were meant to be. Read history and biographies. Emulate heroes. Defend and improve this great experiment named America. Champion the ideas and policies that create incentive, opportunity, enterprise, and growth, because a rising tide lifts all boats. Cherish and commit to our families. And finally, let's all follow the example of the Good Shepherd, who left the ninety-nine to go after the one.

One of my dad's closest friends, allies, and intellectual sparring partners was his former presidential cabinet teammate, Bill Bennett. It was Bill who first expressed to me the meaning behind LIFT when describing my father.

After Dad's memorial service, Bill and his wife, Elayne, came by my mother's home, where family and friends had gathered, and regaled us with humorous and resounding memories of Dad. Bill summed it all up by saying something to the effect that, "Wherever Jack went, wherever he spoke, whomever he met, whatever the issue, Jack Kemp brought LIFT—to huddles, to ideas, to people, to politics, to our nation."

What Bill was identifying was that his friend strove to inspire and elevate others to be their best. Jack Kemp passed along a legacy of perseverance, leadership, and encouragement. He taught us how to find ways to bring something very good out of very bad situations. He was an optimist and an encourager. He modeled his deeply held belief that we must champion opportunity, good ideas, and policies, not solely for our own sake, but most of all, on behalf of the disenfranchised, those left behind. That's authentic, dynamic, and transformational leadership.

John F. Kennedy coined the phrase "A rising tide lifts all boats." He was describing the value of stimulating the economy by reducing tax rates for people and businesses at every level of our economy, the wealthy as well as those earning comparatively little. He believed, as did my father, that if the economic tide rises, the economy will grow, more profits will be made, more jobs will be created, fewer will depend on government spending, tax revenues will increase, and every person, rich or poor, will benefit. The measure of success won't be how much money is paid out toward welfare, but rather how few people depend on welfare as they're lifted out of poverty. The poor shouldn't have to stay poor. The rich need not be punished.

This philosophy of LIFT isn't just true on a macro level, but on a micro level as well. Some view success as an individual pursuit. I believe true success involves bringing as many people along as possible, creating a life of LIFT. In this paradigm, leadership isn't just for a chosen few. Everyone is a leader, in one context or another.

My friend Gary Kubiak is the offensive coordinator for the Baltimore Ravens, and former head coach of the Houston Texans. He's a man who knows football inside and out. As a player, he used to be backup quarterback for John Elway. Gary was one of the best sixty quarterbacks in the world, but he typically didn't get to play; he spent most games watching someone *else* play. He received a Super Bowl ring, though his role had been a supporting one. Here are his thoughts on thinking like a leader, even when you don't always feel like one:

> I always thought like a starter, and prepared myself like a starter, although more often than not I was on the sidelines. When I was on the sidelines I understood I was a backup, but the minute I was in the game, I became the starter. In the same way, everyone is a leader because everyone has an influence on some other person. You must always operate under the impression that your actions will influence another.

This breaks leadership out of the realm of power and status and into the realm of relationships and example. It's encouragement, casting vision, and inspiring others. Think about the environments in which you would be considered a leader, perhaps your business environment or your family. Do you fall into the rut of focusing on shortcomings and forget to notice, highlight, and recall the best things? I'm not suggesting we videotape the highlights of our kids, spouses, or employees and show them on Saturday nights. But think of what a great leadership strategy it is to have a highlight night at the dinner or conference table, or to write notes, texts, or emails to affirm and praise our kids, spouses, or employees.

How long has it been since you looked for the positive in someone? If your child's grades are poor or he/she has broken a rule, if an employee has lost a sale or failed to comply with a regulation, is there still something in their character or potential you can highlight and amplify? I guarantee that will produce better results than criticism. When you think of leadership, remember LIFT. Look for the good and highlight it! Call out the best in people, even before they see it in themselves or achieve at that level.

Great Leadership in Action

I've saved an old VHS tape in my home, and the label on it reads simply *Jeff Kemp—Good and Bad*. It's a tape of about twenty plays, pulled from the first three games I quarterbacked during the 1986 season after Joe Montana was injured.

One day, Bill Walsh called me into his office, sat me down next to him, and popped in the videotape. He wanted me to see how I was doing, so that I could improve and help the team grow, win, and fulfill our goals. I'd already seen each of the plays on the tape during our postgame film sessions on Mondays. This was extra credit.

Bill meticulously took me through the plays he'd labeled *good*. Some were great runs and long bombs placed perfectly in the receiver's hands. Some were modest plays where little greatness was apparent, but Bill pointed out the minute details of my foot-work and timing for a hand-off or play-action pass. He affirmed me and even commented on one play that "Joe doesn't do it any better than this." That remark made me feel pretty good! As a leader who *lifts*, Bill was hunting for the treasures and strengths in my playing. He affirmed and highlighted them, which gave me confidence and hope. It raised my standards.

Then, just as meticulously, he took me through the plays labeled *bad*. He pulled no punches, explaining what was wrong, how I could improve, and why it had to be better. I've never been more receptive to coaching or motivated to improve as I was after that session with Bill. He reviewed my good AND my bad, and painted a picture of how I could do even better.

Great leadership is coaching, not bossing. It's mentoring, not managing. It's serving, not being served. It's casting vision for what people can be, not limiting people to definitions of what they were or how they've fallen short. Leadership must make reality known and then help people face it. Yet how that's done is a matter of huge variation in both style and impact.

Some people can deliver truth, but do so with no love or grace or respect—with little to no sense of affirmation and encouragement for growth and progress. Many people can give kindness, grace, and affirmation, but they can't fully deliver what is best for others because they can't present the truth. Great leadership—true leadership—does both. The best coaches and leaders, the best teachers and mentors, the best bosses, politicians, rabbis, priests, and pastors, the best friends, the best parents, the best spouses . . . they share the precious balance of truth and love, of reality and encouragement.

I see this in my wife, Stacy, and her wonderful style of parenting our children. She demonstrates and communicates tons of love and mixes it continually with the gift of truth, graciously presenting reality. I have grown from my living with her, and my sons have been profoundly and positively shaped by her large doses of love and truth.

I remember another powerful instance of great leadership by a coach. In 1984, I was several games into my first year as a starting quarterback in the NFL. We had a running attack, built around the Hall of Fame phenomenon Eric Dickerson, and a huge line. My role was to hand off to Eric, throw short passes and long bombs, scramble out of trouble, and protect the football by avoiding turnovers. (Eric would run for 2,105 yards that year, an epic record and feat.)

Weeks into the season, we were winning and yet I was throwing fewer passes than any quarterback in the league. Coach Robinson called me into his office to reassure me there was no lack of confidence in, or importance to, my role, despite what might be written in the press. He sat me down and slid a sheet of paper across his desk with a few stats written on it. First, it listed the very small number of interceptions I'd thrown. "Impressive," he said.

Beside that column was another, a ratio of touchdown passes to number of passes attempted. He told me these numbers were also admirable. In fact, it was the highest ratio among NFL quarterbacks at that point in the season. Then he pointed out our win-loss record, an impressive one under my short tenure as a new starting quarterback. That was the most important stat, he reminded me.

That meeting was a major boost for me, just as the Walsh meeting would be two years later. John Robinson still eventually traded and replaced me. However, he showed me a valuable way to show players that what they do is crucial because of how it relates to the *team's* success, not just their own *personal* (and smaller) definition of success.

LIFT Leadership Leads

Another important component of great leadership is that it doesn't leave people where they are; it takes them somewhere. As someone once said, "If no one's following, you're not really leading."

In the same way, LIFT takes people from one state of being to another. It's not just imparting a fun disposition to people or giving them a kick in the pants. When you live a life of LIFT, you coach, you encourage, you heal, you transform. You help people go from immature to mature. You help them move from what is far from complete to what is more complete, from what is disintegrated to being integrated. Sometimes you take them from broken to whole. You become part of other people's restoration process, lifting them out of their blitzes and inspiring a larger vision. You help them become even better versions of themselves—what they were intended to be.

Does this sound presumptuous? It's not meant that way. That's because authentic and transformative leadership is, before anything else, humble. Humility is the fulcrum of whether things go positive or negative, whether people come together or are torn apart. Humility is the character trait that opens the door through which everything else that's good can flow.

My friend Rich Begert is a CEO whose background includes running wireless industry companies and large construction companies. Rich is tall, confident, and bold. Early in his career, a leadership consultant pegged him as being arrogant. Rich listened and took the frank assessment to heart. Today, he's a leader whose style is marked by humility. Despite a busy schedule and heavy demands, he frequently goes into work in the mornings and loads the dishwasher, takes out the trash, and puts on the coffee. His employees catch him doing these things and ask, "Why are you doing that?"

He responds, "Why not? It needs to be done."

He doesn't make a big deal about it. He washes dishes in his own home too, not as a duty but with joy, because it makes his wife feel loved, and it contributes to the good of the family.

That's authentic humility. That's the kind of leader people *want* to follow, the kind of leader who lifts people through the power of example.

In his business book *Good to Great*, author Jim Collins identifies what he calls "Level Five leaders," those who carry their organization past the level of *good* performance to *great* performance.

Guess what he identifies as these leaders' number one quality? Humility!

These successful leaders may be dogged and focused, but they're first of all humble—humble enough to admit they aren't perfect. Humble enough to serve their teams and lead by example. Humble enough to be self-examining, evaluating, changing, and reinventing. Humble enough to focus on and lift others.

LIFT Leadership Serves

This kind of leadership has sometimes been called "servant leadership." Servant leadership, proponents say, is the most effective and fulfilling influence, whether you're leading a team, a family, a business, a nonprofit, a nation, or any group. I agree.

> Not everyone can be famous, but everyone can be great, because greatness is determined by service.
>
> Dr. Martin Luther King Jr.

Great leadership serves others and adds value to their lives, in a manner that causes them to repeat it and "pay it forward." Empower them. Equip them. Turn them into leaders who lift others. It's multiplication, not addition. Again, it's the power of humility and example, which leads to success in *others*, not just in the leaders themselves. Great leadership serves. The greatest leadership replicates by creating other servant leaders.

Frosty Westering, the late famed college football coach, was an eccentric and renowned Division III champion. He was a servant-leader coach who has literally hundreds of disciples carrying out his coaching philosophy today. Under Frosty's leadership style of humility and positive example, scores of young men learned to use coaching and sports to build a platform for blessing others. They're continuing his legacy of building bonds of love and loyalty, which are often missing characteristics of real manhood. Over the years, these young men have moved on into careers across all sectors of life throughout the country, from doctors and lawyers to teachers and entrepreneurs. An overwhelming number of them have gone into the public schools and sports (many on a volunteer basis) as coaches themselves, working to raise up a generation of young athletes who demonstrate what they were taught:

1. Character that values others (selflessness).
2. Care and concern for people around them (goodness).
3. Leadership as servanthood (leading by humility, example, and others-centeredness).

Rich Begert, whom I mentioned earlier, engendered trust and respect for his messages and leadership, because he proved that he served and cared for his people in practical ways. Additionally, in his regular Friday staff meetings, he would open himself to concerns and questions from his team. "How can I serve you?" he would ask. Can you envision the kind of buy-in, honesty, and commitment Rich received from his team because of the way he modeled servant leadership to them?

People like Rich and Frosty are leaders who invest. They're not consuming from their employees and teams or treating them as a resource to be used. They see their teams as *people*—people lifted to be the best they can be, for their own good and for the mutual good of the team.

> The Son of Man did not come to be served, but to serve, and to give his life as a ransom for many.
>
> Matthew 20:28

Sadly, in our culture today, humility and others-centeredness are often viewed through a skeptical or even negative lens. But if you decide to embrace lifting others as a lifestyle, you'll find it's a great joy to *choose* to position yourself so that someone else can be served, elevated, and empowered.

Norm Evans was an All-Pro member of the "perfect season" 1973 Miami Dolphins. He's a great leader who built and ran Pro Athletes Outreach, a conference ministry to help pro athletes and spouses build solid spiritual, marital, and lifestyle foundations under their lofty and precarious careers. One of the reasons I ran my own organization, and love to see other people grow, is that Norm did that for me. He was the natural emcee and leader of his organization, but he took a backseat on the podium. He always pushed young players with leadership potential into the speaker/leader role. His joy was to see us develop into leaders rather than doing the up-front leadership himself, something he could do better than us.

My friend and executive coach, Scott Sticksel, once challenged me to seek to "out-bless others" in my every interaction. To be honest, I wasn't ready yet to assimilate that message. I was hoping for great things to happen for ME in relationships! Today, however, the liberating truth of this approach to life is increasingly validated, even though I'm no model of consistency. There's something incredibly freeing and empowering about not always having to protect and promote yourself. Sure, it's countercultural; after all, we're me-centered humans in a rights-based consumer society. Aiming at the best for others . . .

It's vulnerable.
It's counterintuitive.
But it's effective.

It's powerful.
It's uniting.
It's transformative.

It's LIFT.

LIFT Leadership Influences

As foolish as it might seem, one of a leader's best sources of building credible influence is with his/her own weakness. That's where authentic humility becomes leverage. Let people know you're real by demonstrating an awareness of your weaknesses. Share with them a story of your biggest blitz(es) in life. You'll be surprised at how this lowers people's guards and builds a deeper connection. Step off your pedestal. In doing so, you make yourself more believable and trustworthy. Leaders already have the power position. To lead well, what's needed more than anything is trust.

It's who you are, not just what you achieve, that gives you credibility. And the greatest credibility comes from humility—the honesty to reveal your real, and imperfect, self. Impressive achievements sometimes make people feel they can never live up to or accomplish what you do, or what you expect of them. Don't make it seem as though it's all success, as though it all came so easily. Work alongside your team and show them when you're sweating. Be transparent.

Patrick Lencioni talks about this principle in his book *Getting Naked: A Business Fable.*[1] Transparency, ending the pose that all is easy and fine, is a vital component of building trust—vulnerability-based trust.

This principle goes for parenting too. Parents, let's step off our pedestals. As kids grow older, they won't accept a parent's message if that message is simply being *told to* them. They accept a parent's message through example, especially when it's delivered with humility. When parents come alongside a child in a personal way, revealing their own journeys and failures, they're more empowered to help a child learn valuable life lessons. It's so much better than lecturing or resorting to sending a child off elsewhere to figure life out on his or her own.

Chuck Knox, my Seahawks coach, always used to say, "What you do speaks so loud I don't need to hear what you say." Show me your talent, don't talk about it. Be an example, not a lecture. Present your real self, not an airbrushed Teflon version of yourself. It's true with kids, and it's true with employees; it works anywhere you lead by example. When you share your weaknesses, it makes others feel comfortable in showing theirs. Truth and teamwork become the norm, instead of posing and selfish posturing.

Your employees and your children don't necessarily want you to be a peer relationally, but neither do they want you to be a distant, elevated authority and power. Don't just be a boss; be a model of what you're advocating. Be one who comes alongside. And don't try to come across perfect. That's impossible and it's not credible.

LIFT Leadership Values Interdependence

Granted, to invest in intimate relationships and become interdependent with others involves risk. When you trust in someone, you take the risk that they may break your trust. There's the chance of getting hurt, rejected, disappointed, or even betrayed. But there's also the opportunity to be loved and become a part of something bigger than yourself. There are others in your life with whom to share your burdens and join in your successes, which is much more pleasurable than finding yourself at the top of the success mountain, but alone, with no one there to share the experience with you.

> If we have no peace, it is because we have forgotten that we belong to each other.
>
> Mother Teresa

That's why relationship investors enjoy life more than consumers. When you invest in lifting people, you have more positive, interdependent relationships with people than when you consume their time and talent or simply use them. You'll also have more of a platform on which to speak hope into their lives, the ability to impart great vision, and more opportunities to help them grow, to take on and overcome the blitzes in their lives. Bottom line: As an investor in relationships, you'll increase others' overall effectiveness as well as the satisfaction and trust of your team members.

LIFT Leadership Replicates

Greatness replicates because it inspires, equips, and empowers others in such a way that they want to do the same and pay it forward. I saw this quality in Matt Hasselbeck, a sixteen-plus-year veteran NFL starting quarterback who was demoted by the Tennessee Titans when they chose a young second-year quarterback, Jake Locker, to lead the team. Many observers felt that Jake played no better than Matt, and it was doubtless he would make mistakes and miss opportunities that Matt's experience would have prevented.

Nonetheless, Matt's attitude remained upbeat when interviewed by the media. He admitted he was disappointed that he wasn't named the starter, yet he wasn't daunted by it. His comments were less about his own circumstances and more about how he was "excited" for Jake. Matt made sure that his remarks signified no reluctant acceptance, but rather a team-oriented drive to do all he could to help Jake succeed.

Matt had much veteran experience and coaching to offer a young QB. He gave it to Jake willingly, but he didn't take credit for developing it on his own. He credited NFL commentator and former QB Trent Dilfer, who had done the same for him.

Trent was the QB ahead of Matt early in Matt's career in Seattle. In uncanny similarity, Matt replaced a demoted Trent, and was both surprised and deeply impacted by the way Trent channeled all the disappointment at not playing himself into enthusiasm for preparing and supporting Matt as the new, younger QB. That's an example of paying it forward. Matt served Jake Locker because Trent had served Matt. Then, when a new season approached, and a new team kept Matt's career alive, bringing him in to support and back up Andrew Luck of the Colts.

When the next page in the NFL turns and Jake Locker or Andrew Luck sees his job given to a younger generation QB, I fully expect that because Trent and Matt mentored and encouraged so well, Jake and Andrew will do the same for the guys who follow them. An others-centered teamwork that serves a player taking over your position is a great feat of replication, and a great example of LIFT!

Oh . . . and guess who coached and modeled lift leadership to Trent Dilfer? His former head coach at Tampa Bay, Tony Dungy!

LIFT Leadership Loves

We love because he first loved us.

Apostle John, speaking of Jesus[2]

Most people wouldn't think of "loving" as a high priority and quality for a leader. More often than not, leaders who love are those who have learned to walk in humility, whose regard for self and others was forged in the fire of blitzes. The experience of facing a blitz is precisely what builds our humility, interdependence, empathy, and compassion.

Tony Dungy is a rare leader whose personal care for his players and assistant coaches has become legendary, and was so deep and evident that it generated loyalty and performance. ESPN analyst and former Colt quarterback Brock Huard described Tony's caring nature as being so powerful that players on his team did their utmost not to disappoint him. They didn't need the host of fines and penalties that most teams needed to keep players from being late to meetings or eating their way past their weight targets during the season. Brock told me that because the players respected and loved Tony due to his integrity and love for them, they *didn't need the list of rules and fines.*

What does your spouse really want to know? What do your children, employees, co-workers, or clients want to know? It's "Do you care about me?" That's the key to it all, and our ability to answer this question for them is dependent on whether we take an investor or a consumer mind-set toward life and toward them. How about you? Do you desire what is best for others, and will you do it? That's love. That's the relationship-investor mentality.

Many people tell me they heard this concept frequently in the tone and ideas in my father's speeches and leadership. He framed ideas to trust and empower people, combining the common good with the best of their personal dreams. His optimistic, engaging, and passionate manner celebrated and reached out to people of all backgrounds and walks of life. Dad loved taking interest in young people, underdogs, and those who are often ignored.

I traveled and campaigned with him during the 1996 presidential campaign when he was running for vice-president. He always got roused up for his speeches, but I remember him being even more enthused and passionate when he made special trips through the kitchens of the hotels and restaurants where events were being held. He loved to shake hands and frolic with the chefs and waitstaff. We had more fun in a Memphis hotel kitchen staffed by modestly paid African-American men and women than anywhere else. Thousand-dollar donors would have to wait. He used to show us, and occasionally tell us, "People don't care how much you know until they know how much you care."

Contrary to some traditions and much modern pragmatism, leadership and love are NOT at different ends of the spectrum. They're not inconsistent, incompatible, or from different realms altogether. Good leadership—humane leadership—is love applied on a macro scale.

Power and control may lead in the short term, but a legacy of leadership—the true success of replication—requires more. There is no shortcut around, or replacement for, the power of leading through relationship: caring, knowing, committing, accepting, affirming, encouraging, celebrating, giving, forgiving, inspiring, and growing. It's upon the foundation of care and empathy that the best results come from confronting, challenging, correcting, and disciplining. Together these are love. These are what marks leadership that *lifts*.

LIFT is a style of leadership that lives on, one that leaves a legacy. A legacy is not statistics, assets, notoriety, or records. It's a pattern of lives being lived differently, and love being expressed by others because you loved well and led others to love.

Leaders Who LIFT

A leader is not solely defined by his or her position. Everyone is a leader—even backup quarterbacks. In life, most of us will spend a fair amount of time on the proverbial bench, but that doesn't mean we aren't in the game, as ex-Bronco quarterback Gary Kubiak illustrated for us earlier in this chapter. We are constantly shaping and influencing the lives of other people. Many times it's people we don't even know we're impacting.

> The most important thing a coach or leader does is make sure that every single teammate and coach knows how important and necessary he is to the team.
>
> Mike Swider,
> Head Football Coach,
> Wheaton College, Illinois

Remember, you don't need to be a "first-stringer" to have an impact. I wasn't Joe Montana. I wasn't John Elway. Still, there were things I could do as a backup quarterback to help my team and teammates.

I could be a role model of preparation and commitment, inspiring others to give their very best effort. When a young player confided that he had marital problems, I could share the difficulties that Stacy and I had faced and what I'd learned about commitment and about God's help in times of trouble. When a rookie was paralyzed with fear that he was going to be cut, I could offer him encouragement: "Hey, I saw how well you ran today. I know what you can do. You have a good chance!" As Stacy often pointed out to me, focusing on encouraging others also kept my mind off my problems and the stress of surviving each summer's roster cuts myself!

Bottom line: Great leadership that encourages others to be all they were designed to be is simply *influence that serves.* To achieve it, we need to wake up to the poison of our consumer culture and self-concerned, self-serving society. Otherwise we'll deceive ourselves, live for self, and miss our calling and our joy—that of living a life of LIFT.

Time Out for Self-Reflection

Consider your attitude toward your team—your marriage, your family, your department, or your company:

- Are you looking to take from them or to give to them?

- Do you want to impress them or empower them?

- Are your communications a transaction of information or a touching of hearts?

- Do you place yourself above those who want to listen to you, and above those who must listen to you?

- Do you let leadership, status, fame, or any form of power change your view of yourself and others so that a hierarchy or ranking exists?

- Have you seen experts or speakers who "fly in and fly out," who left an event early and never bothered to connect with individuals at the event where they spoke? Would that be your tendency?

- Consider the times when your thoughts about a particular person were dominated by wanting the best for them, their growth, their advancement, their success, and their joy. Remember the times when you were able to inspire, encourage, or lift someone to be a better version of themselves. Why not make it your aim to do that all the time, with all people, even when they frustrate or don't reciprocate your love and concern?

In your worst moments, when you are fatigued and spent, what is the character *you* demonstrate? What is your leadership LIFT quotient?

Run the Play: Practical Application

Life, Lift, Leverage: 36 Nuggets of Wisdom for Servant Leaders

1. Recognize you're in your right place. This prevents anxious, self-centered striving.

2. Know that you go nowhere by accident, meet no one by accident, and nothing happens by accident.

3. Be committed to the truth that right is right, even if no one is doing it, and that wrong is wrong, even if everyone is doing it.

4. Treat all people the way you would like to be treated if you were in their shoes.

5. Forgive as you wish to be forgiven.

6. Be the first to apologize if you wish to heal broken relationships.

7. Do the right thing, especially when no one is looking.

8. Recognize problems as opportunities, disguised as impossible situations.

9. Speak the same positive message with your actions, body language, tone, and words.

10. Be like the eagle, not the buffalo. Lead and soar; don't follow the herd.

11. Recognize that life is not a zero-sum game. Being generous and creative expands the pie for everyone.

12. See your marriage as a contest of generosity.

13. Remember that in marriage, when a couple argues, if either person aims to win, both lose.

14. See love as a decision, a series of choices. Desire and do what's best for the other person.

15. Give yourself the gift of forgiving others. Free yourself of the chains of bitterness.

16. Be curious, study hard, and always be prepared. Chance favors those who are prepared.

17. Embrace the adage "Much can be accomplished when there's little concern for who gets the credit."

18. Realize you're never as good as, or as bad as, they say you are. Don't live for the approval of the audience and particularly the media. Fame is a counterfeit to real life.

19. Live to out-bless others in every interaction.

20. Look people in the eye. Repeat their names to yourself. Ask them questions to learn something about them. Be interested, not interesting.

21. To belong, make others feel they belong.

22. To make friends, be friendly to others.

23. Remember that a true friend remains loyal when trouble and failure come.

24. Defeat your enemies by making them your friends or by dropping the fight.

25. Recognize that ideas have consequences. Pay attention to truth. Learn how to explain ideas to skeptics, not to those who already agree with you. Make your ideas simple; base them in compassion and reality.

26. Look for the positive, seeing more of what is good in people and situations.

27. Expect more of yourself than of others.

28. Don't give up on yourself or other people.

29. Focus, focus, focus. Priorities mean saying no to good things and saying yes to best things.

30. Search for God. We were designed to be fully satisfied only by Him. Learn contentment. In the words of American Orthodox rabbi Daniel Lapin, "Regardless of how much we possess, we are created with a drive to want even more."

31. Be responsible and honest. Our actions can unintentionally harm our children's lives.

32. Have the courage to say what needs to be said. Jim Barksdale once declared, "The toughest conversations to have are usually the most helpful and constructive."

33. Seek integrity in an employer and give others that same privilege.

34. Hire people smarter than you, with gifts you don't have.

35. Beware of power and fame. Stay humble. Max De Pree said, "Leadership is abandoning yourself to the strengths of others."

36. Have vision for what others can be, especially your spouse and children. See more than their behavior; see their potential and strengths, and bolster the best in their character. Speak it into them before it's fully apparent.

Pick three of the above to work on this week. Write them down and post them wherever you'll see them as a reminder. The following week, pick three more. Write your own Nuggets to help you serve, lead, and lift others!

9

Strengthen Your Marriage

A good marriage is a contest of generosity.
                                        Diane Sawyer

I know a couple whose only personality similarity is that they're both competitive and dominant leaders. He's a spontaneous, impulsive, fun-seeking extrovert who is into pleasing people and has a strong wiring to "feel and perceive" things. She's an orderly, responsible introvert who has a strong moral compass and is wired to "think through the facts" about things. This man went into marriage naïvely thinking it would be easy and automatic. Not seeing his self-referential immaturity, he thought, *I'm a great guy. She'll be happy with me, and she'll love making me happy.*

Much like (okay . . . exactly like) these two people, my wife, Stacy, and I started out thrilled with each other, expecting married life to be natural because we were so committed. We didn't set out to make marriage a contest of personalities or to compete with each other, but we very naturally and unpleasantly gravitated to that. We each saw our perspective and way of doing things as "right," as the way things "ought to be." We each had a tendency to hold our opinion, argue our point, act defensively, and steal much joy and harmony from each other and ourselves. Our commitment and both our journeys to know and love God made us seek to learn and grow and improve. We had to! Our journey has humbled us, changed us, and deepened our vision of marriage. We've grown so much but are not fully free from this weakness, even today.

Our five-year-old son, Keegan, heard us having a disagreement one day. He looked up at me and said, "Daddy, you and Mommy are too different to be married." Whoa. I was a bit rocked and knew it was a teachable moment. The pressure was on. I rallied and got down on my knee, looking him in the eye. "No, Keegan, the reason Mommy and Daddy *are* married is because we are so different."

I went on to explain how football teams need very opposite players to complement each other—huge linemen, lightning-quick running backs, etc. I explained how men and women are opposite and that people with different personalities often team up, which is good for partnership and teamwork. Then I reassured him we'd stay together by reminding him, "We've got God to glue us together." I thought it was a pretty good marriage speech until Keegan replied, "Well, Dad, with you guys it's gonna take Krazy Glue!"

Granted, Stacy and I are incredibly different in personality styles. While we've certainly had a great deal of joy and adventure, we've also experienced friction and frustration. Our extremely opposite giftings create potential to be a powerful team with a complementary range of perspective and style. We haven't learned to think alike. We're still different. But we do know how the other thinks, and we've learned to be less frustrated by that. In fact, usually we can see the value in it. More and more we see the humor in it! And that improves marriage and life.

Over time, with experience, effort, and practice, a married couple can learn to understand each other, think jointly, and grow together. They can face and overcome blitzes together because they have become, essentially, the *ultimate team*.

Marriage as the Ultimate Team

Marriage is not for the faint of heart. It's a promise bigger than the two people who marry. It's a serious, dedicated covenant to forge a lifetime bond. You need to know what the promise is if you want to make it work. It's an institution we join, not solely a private relationship. It's meant to shape us, improve us, and call out the best in us.

It seems like common sense that a marriage ought to function like a team, doesn't it? Yet so many people don't see it, leaving them to drift from that ideal. Wanting what I want, and wanting to dictate the terms of the relationship, is par for the course for us postmodern people, especially Americans. It's also where marriage seems to go wrong on the road to decay.

For some, marriage is a love depot—a place to *get* love—which isn't very sustainable, when people are focused on taking rather than giving. This is consuming rather than investing, focused on self rather than on the couple—the team. Feeling unloved from your childhood and not loving yourself can be a setup for disappointment when marriage is viewed as an idealistic remedy for the hole in your heart.

For some it's a partnership—efficient for taking care of life's economic and practical details, but lacking in intimacy, romance, shared joy, and spiritual advancement. For others, marriage can be a competition, filled with frequent quips, bickering, battles, and arguments to prove who is "right," who is "in charge," and whose personality is correct. Some see marriage as a project to change another person into the spouse or parent one wants them to be. This is dishonoring, counterproductive, and frustrating—a formula for disaster. Again it springs from the mind-set of a consumer.

These are not the only obstacles. Sadly, there's been a widespread, cultural blitz on marriages and families. Frequent divorces and fractured families. Fear of commitment and the risk of splitting. It's been a blitz on the social, economic, and moral supports to crucial building-block institutions. But no matter the cultural swings and troubling trends, the essence of marriage represents something written on the human heart: the desire for love, companionship, loyalty, and a completing partnership.

No human bond is more basic, more diverse, more beautiful, more creative, or more essential to creating and nurturing life (including children who are loved and raised by their biological or adoptive mother and father) than marriage. Unselfish commitment and love for another who is different but complementary to you is a picture of God's loyal commitment and love. It's so heartbreaking that we imperfect and selfish humans, and our often corrosive and individualistic society, have weakened the very thing that's meant to bring out the best in adults, give the best to children, and reflect the love of our Creator.

As painful as the family landscape can be today, hope still exists. There are millions of strong, happy, resilient marriages. And though not visibly marketed or portrayed, a myriad of support efforts and training resources exist to help heal hurting marriages. There's proof of this hope—my own marriage is an example of that.

I say that with humor because I know as much as anyone that it's not easy and we're still thousands of miles from perfect. In fact, years ago, when Stacy and I were asked to lead a group of married couples at our church, we asked, "Why *us*?"

The pastor chuckled and said, "Because if YOU GUYS can make it, anyone can!"

Time, practice, commitment, and experience—among other things—have taught Stacy and me to think and behave differently than when we first married. And after thirty years of marriage, despite our differences and weaknesses, we have become an ultimate team. We're a complementary team, committed to unity in the most important roles we'll ever have in life.

Marriage Requires Teamwork

As I shared with Keegan, football teams are made up of players with different body types, shapes, and talents. You've got big and powerful linemen, sleek and tall receivers, tough and flashy running backs, discerning and nervy quarterbacks who lead the team and throw the ball. None of them can do what the others do. The team does best when each player focuses on and performs his assigned role.

Having diverse strengths implies having differences and weaknesses. People with different strengths may look at other people's makeups as faults. We look at the world through biased lenses. This is a reality for a sports team, a business team, or a marriage team. Good teams, however, don't point out each other's weaknesses; they spend their time coordinating their strengths. They also learn to serve one another for mutual success. Quarterbacks are taught to serve the receivers, and the receivers are instructed to serve the quarterback, not to expect the other to serve them! The team benefits when QBs focus on being as accurate as possible for receivers, while receivers focus on catching anything they can touch.

Individuals—whether teammates or marriage partners—must learn to sacrifice to be their best so that they can make the *team* shine, not themselves. In fact, when an athlete or teammate allows their focus to drift to such things as selfish rewards, personal statistics, and credit for their role, that's arrogance—unhealthy pride. It's self-centered, not team-centered. Self-centeredness will damage cohesiveness, which ultimately reduces the achievements and joys available to the whole team.

Good teamwork, then, requires making yourself compatible with others instead of focusing on how the other can become more compatible to you. It's looking to your *own* responsibility, not taking an online inventory at a dating site to seek out the easiest person with whom to get along, one who will not stretch and diversify your view and approach to life. Good teamwork requires personal growth, an others-centered orientation toward companionship, nearness, involvement, and cooperation.

Good teamwork also means being joined at the heart and soul, as well as at the hip. Since we humans are souls with bodies and not bodies with souls, this becomes one vital area for strong alignment. If a couple has shared spiritual beliefs or religious practices, this makes the cohesiveness all the stronger. It's so much easier and constructive to have the same faith as an anchor and framework, a source of love and forgiveness, a lodestar for raising your children, for facing eternity. To share spiritual life with your mate enriches the marriage. To lack that ability and passion creates an imbalance of sorts.

Couples who make their belief in God an active part of their life, who see God through the lens of having a relationship with Him, will find that their team includes His presence in a bonding and empowering manner. They'll find spiritual richness in the process of uniting, surrendering themselves, and serving another person—relationally, spiritually, and sexually.

This is the added bonus to the marriage team. While similar to other kinds of teams, happy husbands and wives do not operate like companies, soldiers, coaches, or sports teams. They don't operate on power. They don't operate on authority. They operate on *love*. Commitment, affection, sacrifice, forgiveness, and loyalty . . . love.

A Team for Life

Another unique feature of the marriage team is that it's a team for life, and a team for a lifetime. To be married means to "covenant" yourself together, to be yoked or woven together as one made up of two. It takes agreement to the nature of marriage, to the lifetime of marriage, to the *loyalty* of marriage.

Loyalty is comprehensive. It means considering and caring for the interests of the other in sexual expression and bonding. This means blessing—not taking from or neglecting—the other. It means honoring fidelity (faithfulness) in every sense. Your spouse is your *one and only* in every respect: sexually, emotionally, visually, and mentally. This means saying no to comparing, ogling, imagining, or lusting after anyone other than your spouse. It means committing to being emotionally, financially, and physically dedicated to the team.

Being joined in marriage requires agreement. It demands teamwork, consideration, communication, consultation, cooperation, compromise, and companionship. Without these essentials, the marriage team simply cannot and will not function well. A team consists of people working together, yoked together, coupled, linked, and cooperating for the common good. When Webster's Dictionary defines the word *yoked*, it uses marriage to illustrate the meaning!

The biblical account of creation describes man and woman as designed and created with similarity and uniqueness, allowing them to complement each other. The text describes the Creator's response to all that He created as, "It was good."[1] But one thing stood out as not being good. That was the condition of being alone. We read, "The Lord God said, 'It is not good for the man to be alone. I will make a helper suitable for him.'"[2]

The team could not consist of one, physiologically or relationally. The ultimate team needs biological capacity to replicate. It needs to represent all of humanity, both male and female, and so needs to represent both aspects of God's image. He explained that He created us in His image, again male and female, both of which bear certain aspects, but not all, of the image of God. Evidently, God must be like women in some ways and like men in others. God must be relational in ways that are represented by the bonded and complementary relationship of a husband and wife. Marriage is meant to paint a picture of a relational God, who sacrificed and raised His most valued Son to bond with those He loved.

The marriage team naturally draws one who is highly attuned to nurture, nesting, and relational security. But the team also needs one who is highly attuned to task, encouraging adventure, and engagement with the outer world. My own marriage dynamic is somewhat humorous in that my personality is closer to the female generalization of being more feelings-based, emotional, and sentimental. My wife has distinct leadership characteristics and is a thinker far more than a feeler. She's objective, disciplined, organized, and task-oriented. I on the other hand am subjective, spontaneous, relationship-driven, and gifted at disorganizing. (I'm not comparing myself to any gender here!)

She manages well. I dream well. And yet I am the risk-taker, adventure-seeker, and encourager, pushing the kids to stretch their wings. We know ourselves. Our marriage team works well because of that complementary approach to life. That's how we approach the raising and launching of our kids. Together we've been able to grow and release them to be their own selves, young adults living their own lives. Their independence and ownership proves especially essential when they form a new and preeminent family that supersedes our family—their own, new ultimate team.

Melting Selfishness, Molding Love

The marriage team is an identity that doesn't erase the identities of the individuals, but transcends and brings more meaning and richness. It places more demands on the self to grow and mature and excel. No doubt, if you marry and haven't already discovered this, you will!

I interviewed marriage and family experts Dennis and Barbara Rainey, leaders of FamilyLife,[3] on their fortieth wedding anniversary. When I asked Barbara the greatest lesson from her marriage, she shared that marriage has revealed and challenged her selfishness. How honest and wise! From the engagement and wedding forward, your selfishness will be constantly exposed and challenged. Your perspective and approach to things will be tempered and refined. You'll be called on to assist the team, and your approach will need to be bridled to respect and harmonize with your teammate.

Imagine if we were all patient, kind, generous, non-defensive, pure, forgiving, truth-telling, and secure. Imagine if we were impartial, just, open-minded, and compassionate. Imagine giving dignity to every person and distinguishing behavior from person-hood. Gracious, but courageous. Fun, but not frivolous. Pure, but not self-righteous. Discerning, but not judgmental. Forgiving, but not lax. Such a character would purify our motives. We would love ourselves, love others, and sacrifice our interests to elevate and redeem others. That kind of love is what builds and matures in the ultimate team.

Consumer vs. Investor in Marriage

When it comes to your marriage (or your approach to relationships and dating), are you a casual consumer or a committed investor? Are you focused on yourself and what you deserve and want, or are you focused on the other person's needs and wishes?

Commitment and investment improve your situation. A consumer approach, on the other hand, does something selfish and short term to your character. It hinders respect and love. It frustrates relationships. It backfires. Commitment to *marriage* improves both the individuals and the relationship. Commitment to *self* reinforces a consumer approach, discouraging self-improvement and marital growth.

Years ago, when trends shifted to, "Let's just live together and see if we're compatible," researchers expected cohabitation to reduce divorce by helping couples shop well and practice better for marriage. They were wrong.[4]

It turns out that living together *without* a commitment cannot simulate living *with* a commitment. It may even undermine the trust and effort both partners put into their relationship. When you feel you can simply leave if it doesn't work out well, that tends toward your not working as intently in the relationship. It trains couples to hold back on each other rather than give more of themselves to their partner. Partners become objectified as a result, judged by whether they provide the expected amount of satisfaction to the relationship.

Let's face it: The consumer age in which we live has produced failed marriages, broken families, and wounded children. Love has declined and been changed from commitment to feeling—and feelings fluctuate. Building marriages and homes on the sands of feelings hasn't helped us to weather life's storms. We've consumed, rather than invested. But we can do better! Love is not the servant of our fleeting emotions or our fluctuating hormones. *Love* carries the ability to prioritize another person and do what's best for him or her.

My young friend Jeremy to whom I referred earlier had been married just a year when he explained to me what his generation is experiencing and what they think about marriage. What Jeremy told me isn't only applicable to Millennials; it goes for all of us. It just happens that the cultural heat has been turned up more for his generation. He said:

> In my experience, the fear of divorce is very real in the minds of Generation Y/Millennials. Many have seen their parents, friends' parents, or close family members go through divorce—adults they look up to, admire, and trust. The inevitable question they ask is, "If they couldn't do it, what makes me think I can?"
>
> I think one of the major challenges for my generation is consumerism. We have grown up in a country that has known incredible prosperity and freedom, and we have been inundated with advertisements since we were born. We are the customers, and the customers are always right. We've been taught by society not to be satisfied with what we have. We need to update and upgrade constantly or we become outdated and irrelevant. Most of us have never had to learn how to be content.
>
> Most of us would never admit to thinking like consumers, but it remains at the core of our culture and at the foundation of our society. It's almost impossible to be unaffected by it and not let it spill over into our marriages.
>
> If you've never learned how to be content, how to stay committed to something despite how it feels, it will be that much harder to succeed in marriage. The mind-set of marriage is at odds with the

mind-set of consumerism. Unless we make a blatant effort to view our spouse differently than we have been taught to view everything else, we'll slip back into our consumer-focused behavior without even knowing it.

What can we do to help change things? Talk openly about some of the major reasons people get divorced and how those things can be avoided or overcome. As for consumerism, we have to realize that marriage isn't about getting and taking; it's about giving, exchanging. It's not anchored in what you feel; it's anchored in what you believe and who you're committed to. It's not self-focused, it's self-sacrificing. By doing this, we can really improve the chances of successful marriages for Generation Y.

The consumer mind-set expects things. It expends energy on what *we* will get from *others*. The dating scene often develops this, as you're looking FOR something more than you're looking to BE something and GIVE something to another person. Our culture also sets us up for this because of all the advertising that conditions us to believe we deserve to be catered to, always getting the best, that we shouldn't settle for anything less. Trade up. Swap out and buy new. The trophy wife syndrome.

Popular reality shows like the *The Bachelor* and *The Bachelorette* are based on the premise of women and men competing to win favor. The bachelor or bachelorette is the ultimate consumer of the best *prospects*—testing out and jump-starting romance and attraction with multiple people. Then, by comparison and contrast, the star eliminates different prospects until he or she narrows it to the best choice for them. A comprehensive product line to test and choose. How's that for the ultimate in consumer relationships? Yet millions of us watch these shows, and whether we mock it or love it, some of it seeps into our subconscious.

The track record for success after a process like that is very weak. Our cultural climate makes it even tougher, because kids are seeing (and concluding) that the point of relationships is to satisfy oneself. It's to the point that breakups are often done by text message! If relationships don't satisfy, then you move on. Instead of examining *yourself* to become a more loving and considerate person, you dissect and discard others. Instead of giving of *yourself* to build value in the other person and bring out the best in them, you expect the other to meet your needs first and foremost.

Looking for a way out of this destructive mind-set, my friend Mike put a little piece of paper on his bathroom mirror where he would see it daily, which read: *Would I want to be married to me?* It's a reminder to think like an investor and to make his wife's marriage experience the best one possible. He looks to himself and his own responsibility, rather than asking the consumer-based question, Do I want to be married to *her?*

Would I want to be married to me? is an investor question, orienting you to add value to the relationship. The more you ask it, the more you make the other person happy. The more you do that, the more likely it is that the other person will want to show kindness and generosity to you. It's a wise man or woman who invests in the places that most impact his or her life, the places that will generate the greatest rate of return. In relationships, that place to invest is in meeting the deepest needs of others.

Marriage Consumer Quiz

(For Relationship Consumer Quiz, singles may substitute "partner" for "spouse"):

1. Do I sometimes compare my spouse unfavorably to others?
2. Do I focus more on my spouse's faults than my own?
3. How often do I focus on my spouse not meeting my needs rather than how I'm not meeting his/hers?
4. Do I keep score . . . adding up when I do good things and when my spouse doesn't, as well as his or her negatives?
5. Am I impatient with my spouse, quickly upset when he or she doesn't communicate or act as I expect?
6. Do I often complain about or criticize my spouse?

7. When I come home or expect my spouse to arrive home, am I thinking more about what I want him or her to do for me rather than what I will do for them?

8. Do I expect apologies from my spouse but rarely apologize myself?

If you answered yes to any of those questions, you've just been given a valuable wakeup call. If you want to improve your marriage and bring out the best in your spouse, you have much potential to improve things. Find a way to flip a switch each day, and perhaps right before you come home. It's the switch from a consumer mind-set to that of a relationship investor. If you have children, this is a great opportunity to show them what maturity is—the willingness to make changes and to focus on treating your spouse great, regardless of how they initially treat you. That may be the greatest lesson you ever teach your kids. Building a warm, generous, solid marriage is a crucial investment you make in building your children's sense of security and confidence.[5]

Investment: The Language of Love

Research has illuminated that, for most of us, our deepest needs are to experience being loved and respected.[6] It's a person's personality, tastes, and desires that determine what feels most like love and respect to them. Gary Chapman, in his classic relationship book *The Five Love Languages*, points out that if you were trying to share a thought or feeling with someone and they spoke German and you spoke French, you'd need to translate. Even if you had goodwill toward them, they wouldn't understand. You need to be speaking the same language!

While our four boys were little, our home was an intense place, especially just before dinnertime when I would arrive home. My wife loved investing in our family by creating a great meal every night, but those harried minutes with kids wrestling, toys strewn, and dinner preparations underway were the two-minute drill for her. I would often come home speaking my love languages (affirming words and touch). Sometimes I'd rush by the boys and make a point of seeing her first. I might step over a trash bag placed strategically for me to shuttle to the garage. Then I'd go kiss or hug her and say, "Hey, beautiful." Meanwhile I'd completely missed Stacy's love language, which is service. A kiss and some nice words didn't do much for her in the middle of a two-minute drill with the boys flying around her feet. "Love" to her would have been removing the trash and taking the boys out of the kitchen, giving her a few minutes of peace to get dinner on the table. Stacy needs to be loved, and that can look like mowing the lawn or getting her car serviced without being asked. (Ouch, I'm not very good at that.)

I was kind of slow with picking up her love languages, but it's finally coming. On a drive to a wedding recently, Stacy told me she was uncomfortable with how fast I drove and switched lanes. It made her nervous. "I can't relax," she told me.

I thought I was a good driver; I hadn't crashed in twenty-eight years of marriage. But I decided to drive according to her tastes and not my own—to allow more space between our car and the car ahead, and to slow down. We'd been battling this our whole marriage, but I thought, *How can I show her love in her language if I'm making her uncomfortable?*

I bristle at being corrected, so I came up with a system. I told her, "Just say 'beep' when you think I've crossed your comfort zone, and I'll know to slow down and be more conservative."

She only had to "beep" a couple of times. Considering her feelings and changing my driving style created a very comfortable mood in the car, rather than tension. I'd never realized it before, but when my driving makes Stacy tense, she's not into conversation. But I like to have conversations during car rides, and on this trip we had a fun talk. She even mentioned afterward how nice the drive was! And I appreciated not having tense silence in the car, or complaints and criticism. Even though I drove slower than I prefer, I actually enjoyed it, like she did. For so many years I had defended my right to drive my way, even though it bothered her. Dumb! Choosing to speak her language of love by driving less aggressively worked for us both. So ask your spouse what he or she needs to feel more loved or respected, and then make some changes for the good of your relationship.

Marriages Handle Blitzes Positively

Marriage is awesome for many reasons. But it's hard for one overarching reason: Marriage joins together two flawed and selfish people with their own preferences and their own way of seeing and doing things. Thus . . . conflict! Disagreements. Offenses. Mistakes. Slights. Blowups. Even infidelities. Troubles and isolation grow when couples forget that they are a team of two different people. They become competitors or opponents, waiting for the other person to adjust to them.

I asked respected relationship expert Dr. Gary Oliver for the single most important principle to help married couples succeed. His answer mirrors the perspective we've been developing for facing blitzes: "View conflict as an opportunity to develop intimacy."[7]

If you see conflict as an opportunity to learn about and better understand your spouse, your relationship will grow and you'll manage conflict well. There is an approach to conflict that can disagree but not damage.

Dr. John Gottman, Professor Emeritus at the University of Washington, has researched over seven thousand couples and worked with approximately eight thousand couples. His thirty-five years of research is summarized in two findings:

1. Happily married couples behave like good friends and handle their conflicts in gentle, positive says.
2. Happily married couples are able to repair negative interactions during an argument, and they are able to process negative emotions fully.[8]

To summarize, when facing marital and relationship blitzes, remember that you are on the same team; your spouse is not your opponent. Accept conflict as common to all relationships, and view it as an opportunity to engage, to learn more about the other person as they learn more about you. That's intimacy . . . and it takes effort. The key is to work at being positive toward them by showing appreciation, respect, affection, and humor. Self-control is central to marriage if you don't want to damage your spouse, your relationship . . . and, by implication, yourself. Avoid sarcasm and cutting or mean attacks, like calling your spouse lazy or stupid. Face conflict, but do it as an investor who seeks to bring out the best in your spouse and add value to the relationship. Disagreements, spousal hurts, and arguments are best resolved when each person, or at least one person, sets the tone by seeking to understand the other person before seeking to be understood.

At the start of the conflict (and the end of the day), success in marriage comes down to respectful questions, sincere apologies, and genuine forgiveness. That takes humility, courage, and love. And that's where the power source greater than yourself makes such a difference.

Fueling the Conflict Before Facing It

After the wedding of one of our sons and daughters-in-law, I took a little mistake and turned it into another of my marital blunders. I created a conflict. What happened was silly. I was downstairs and opened a bill. Since my wife handles our bills, I ran upstairs to discuss it with her. I bounded into the room where she was engrossed on the computer. She was re-watching a 600+ slide show of wedding photos to find a particular photo. I interrupted her and when she waved me off, I did not take the clue and told her we could handle this quickly.

Unfortunately, I ignored and flustered her, causing her to lose her place and end the slide show. She was upset and told me so. I justified myself. She reiterated her disappointment. I weakly said, "Sorry." She explained how she felt, and the inconvenience I'd caused. I said, "Don't freak out." Things got worse. Duh!

The conflict was growing and I stood there defending myself in my heart, looking blandly at her, while thinking about how often we have this stupid disagreement. Finally, upset with myself that I made her so upset, but less out of empathy for her than frustration at the pain of the conflict, I zipped my lip and went downstairs.

When I sat in my chair I thought, *That is about the one thousand, nine hundred, forty-eighth time we've had that dumb exchange.* I knew I was pretty responsible, but I hadn't faced it before. I began a conversation with God that went something like this:

God, why does that happen so much? I meant well, but then I offended her, then I hurt her, then I made it worse.

The thought God gave me in return was this: *Jeff, you're more upset that you had the conflict than you are that you inconvenienced her. And you're more upset that you had the conflict than that you then hurt her feelings by defending yourself and showing no real empathy.*

You always want her to adjust and accept you. You ask for less of these instances of offense and conflict, but you should be asking me to help you change. You need to want to not hurt her more than you want to not feel bad that you messed up.

Wow . . . That led to a very introspective and intense prayer time, and a decision. I aimed to change so that I could be a better apologizer, be less defensive, and truly be more interested in Stacy's feelings than my own.

I went upstairs, got down on a knee next to her, and told her I was wrong to not apologize fully at first. I was wrong to not want to hear from her how I had inconvenienced her. I was wrong to defend myself. I did not care for her feelings well, and I want to.

I concluded with four things: "I was wrong. I am sorry. Will you please forgive me? I want to change."

Stacy teared up in a good way and swiftly loved me back with her forgiveness, her own apology, and a hug.

Treasure Your Spouse

My friend Dave Ederer has a unique and valuable perspective on marriage. Nine months after losing his first wife to cancer, Dave returned and spoke to his group of fifty male business peers who met weekly. He told me he cried in front of them a bit more than speaking, but he came to them with a purpose. He described how losing his wife had amplified a core truth in his life: His wife was his "treasure."

He guessed that many of those in the group weren't too happy in their marriages and wouldn't describe their spouse as a treasure. He reminded them that their wives were in fact their greatest treasure, and to the degree that they as men prioritized and cherished their wives, they would blossom as a treasure. He threw the responsibility for a great marriage back onto them. In fact, he said if any of us would look for the positives in our spouses—if we praised and encouraged the best things in them, if we remembered back to why we married them, if we treated them as our first priority and joy, if we apologized to them for letting our love grow stale—then our feelings would start to warm again.

Dave said to the guys, "I bought each of you a rose, a box of chocolates, and a card so that you can write your wife a love note. Tell her she's your treasure and you want to do more to appreciate and love her. Write her the note and go home to give it to her. I urge you to do it immediately. Don't go back to work, or we'll expect you to report next week what was more important than going home to tell your wife you love her."

A day later, Dave received a letter from one of the men. He gushed his thanks to Dave, sharing that when he arrived home, his wife's suitcases were packed to leave him. His note softened her heart enough to convince her that he was truly sorry and really did care for her. He asked if she would agree to work on the marriage with him. The years have now passed and that marriage has been saved. They are together, and changed. Dave's blitz—and his choice to challenge and lift his business peers—turned into an epic turnaround of blessing.

I encourage you: Count your marriage as priceless. See your loved ones as treasures. Look for the treasure in them. *Treat* them like a treasure. Maybe it will start with an apology or a willingness to forgive and stop your bitterness and grumbling. Accept him or her as a gift to appreciate and steward.

Realize that true love is a dedication to prioritize and add value into the life of another. Money can't buy you love, and neither can romantic feelings. Love is a decision followed by thousands of choices. Invest.

Let's go back to Dave for a moment. Do you see something remarkable and powerful in Dave's investor approach to life?

He was blitzed by the tragic loss of his wife to brain cancer. He grieved intensely. He was unafraid to be an authentic man who freely cried in front of his business peers, and he was willing to deal with the painful changes forced upon him by his wife's death.

After Dave took a long-term view of his life and his influence on his peers' lives, and after he gained enough strength to go back to his business peer group, he did so with a focus on blessing them—not talking about himself. He cared for them and acted like a coach to a group that he treated like a team.

Dave was an investor, and not just by purchasing cards and flowers for those men. He invested his very self in helping them value their wives and invest in their own marriage and family.

Is Dave superhuman or perfect? Of course not. He was a man shattered by loss. He cried. He hurt. He stumbled. But he also drew close to God. I know Dave. I've seen him focus upon, depend upon, and grow closer in his relationship to Jesus. He credits Jesus with comforting, healing, and empowering him to face blitzes and positively impact others.

Dave has since married a wonderful woman and teammate. He invests in that treasured woman and relationship, bearing in mind the painful lesson of his prior loss. He has also faced multiple late-stage cancers and surgeries himself. Facing cancer has brought further purpose to Dave's life. He uses his extensive cancer-fighting knowledge and oncology network to help scores of people fight cancer. Dave plays the hand he's dealt. He calls on his team of family, friends, and professionals to face his blitzes. He draws closer to and depends upon God as his ultimate power source. He keeps learning and growing. He focuses on helping others and investing in making life better for others . . . and that helps him view blitzes positively, as opportunities, rather than curses. Like Dave, our life, our marriage, and our blitzes impact other people.

Why Your Marriage Team Matters

Did you know your marriage matters to far more people than just yourself and your immediate family? A lot of the blitzes being faced by businesses these days—high turnover, lack of loyalty, absenteeism, silo thinking, poor ethics, entitlement mentality, and character failure—would benefit from a revitalization of marriage. That's because we all bring more to the table as a whole person, a person who's well in their family and relationships.

Well over a century ago, Friedrich Nietzsche made a dire prediction about the fate of the family. Every millennium, he said, has chosen an ever-smaller organizing unit. Two millennia ago, Jews, Greeks, and Romans put the people, the polls, and the empire first. In the next millennium, the tribe and the clan became the basic units of social life. In the current millennium, the family has emerged as the foundation of society. But this emphasis will not last, Nietzsche predicted. In the course of the twentieth century, "the family will be slowly ground into a random collection of individuals," haphazardly bound together "in the common pursuit of selfish ends" and in the common rejection of the structures and strictures of family, church, state, and civil society. The "raw individual" will be the norm and the nemesis of the next millennium.[9]

I'm not wired as a pessimist, but what we have been experiencing all around us reflects much of what Nietzsche described.

I'll try not to be predictive or prophetic, yet I do think there are pendulum swings in history, and I'm leaning in with many others to help swing back to the family as the first and best building block of society. And there's no shortcut or replacement for the cornerstone of family and the DNA of family health—marriage.

The reality is, your marriage matters—not just to you, not just to your kids, not just to your own family. It matters to your community. It matters to your company and co-workers. It matters to our whole society. You have a greater capacity to respond to life's blitzes when supported by your "ultimate team." Your marriage can lift you, you can lift each other, and together you can lift others around you.

Remember how I described the start of my own marriage as naïve and consumeristic on my part? I'd been on a lot of teams but was not much of a teammate during the first years of our marriage. Fortunately, the fact that we had big differences and too much friction was offset by the fact that we both had super-strong commitment. And that made the difference, because we chose to invest, not complain or back away. Stacy and I read books and went to conferences on marriage with other couples from around the NFL. We had older couples invest in us as our mentors. We found marriage relationship-strengthening resources. We gained vision, perspective, and hope. We developed skills in communicating, working through conflict, accepting our differences, and handling money wisely. Our marriage became good. Not easy, but deep and good.

We wanted others to get hope and help like we were finding, so we invited couples from our team and neighborhood to go through the videos with us. We developed a support team of other couples for our marriage. These people were friends to our marriage, committed to our success as a team, more than just individually. And we became the support system and friends for other couples' marriages, which always tended to boomerang into more benefit in our own relationship.

One more powerful thing has always marked our marriage. Stacy and I, as well as some objective outside relationship experts, don't think our marriage would have survived without a special glue, a deeper bond, a greater power. We've had many frustrating arguments, silent car rides, and wild career blitzes to face. But there's one thing we've done nearly every single day of our lives that deepened our intimacy and grew us together. We pray together. Sometimes it's very brief at bedtime. Sometimes it's spontaneous when a situation, challenge, or great joy arises. Often knowing we'll pray prompts me to apologize before I do it. Turning to God together has been the lifeline of our marriage. It keeps us connected emotionally and invites a greater power and greater love into two people and a preeminent relationship that desperately needs it.

Time Out for Self-Reflection

Evaluate Your Own "Ultimate Team"

If you are married, on a scale of 1 to 10, rate yourself: "How well am I making my marriage and spouse a priority, my treasure?"

Then ask yourself, "What would it take to improve my rating to a 10?"

Now, be brave. In a humble and safe tone, ask your spouse, "On a scale of 1 to 10, how's our marriage relationship doing?" Accept and validate your spouse's answer.

Now ask them what it would take to move it toward a 10? Write down his/her suggestions and make it your personal mission to address them.[10]

Guess what! You've just become other-oriented. You've just become an investor. And you've just made a game plan.

Keep Asking the Question, Consumer or Investor?

Make a new habit to ask yourself this question in the morning, throughout the day, and before you spend an evening or weekend together: "Am I thinking like a consumer or an investor?" After a disappointment or blowup, ask, "How can I quit my dumb consumer ways and be an investor?"

Run the Play: Practical Application

Action Steps for Building Your Ultimate Team

1. For those thinking or planning to get married: Put more effort into preparing for, learning about, and growing the relationship than you put into the wedding, the honeymoon, or the appearance of looking like a happy couple. Parties, posing, and pretending do not make a marriage. Commit to efforts to grow communication, empathy, forgiveness, serving, and unity. Find a mentor couple, attend a marriage conference together, and get in-depth premarital counseling.

2. Be intentional about your marriage, about your family, about your relationships. Think of your spouse as your intimate ally. Talk with him/her about anything. Get started being transparent and keeping nothing hidden (even the embarrassing or sensitive things, like sexual-related things) from him/her. Don't ever let walls build up. (Tearing down the walls that grew may be delicate and dangerous work, requiring the help of a counselor, pastor, or mentor couple.) Begin to pray together each day.

3. Listen to your spouse. Be careful how you talk to him/her. Listen and think before you speak. Your words shape and impact your spouse's heart. (Researchers of lasting marriages report that it takes five to eight positives to counter one negative verbal interaction.[11]) You'll reap what you sow.

4. Call home every day from work or travel. Text or do something to let your spouse know that he/she is on your mind above everything else—work, play, or mission. Provide daily communication. Ask questions about what matters to him or her.

5. Be a napkin-note person: Leave sticky-note messages or love notes. Put sweet, encouraging words into his/her life by placing them on the mirror or dashboard or in the mail.

6. Don't ever argue to win. If anyone ever tries to win in marriage, both lose. Only argue to resolve, to settle, to regain peace and unity. Your spouse is not your opponent. Defend the team, not yourself.

7. Approach conflict to grow intimacy. Don't avoid or attack. Ask, "Help me understand (your experience, your view, your feelings, your desires, your fears . . .)."

8. Practice love's powerful words: "I was wrong." "I am sorry." "Please forgive me." "I was hurt." "I forgive you."

9. Affirm your wife or husband. This cannot be overdone! Don't be lax. To criticize or demean them is to shoot yourself in the foot, to damage yourself. Think. Praise. Admire. Encourage. Affirm.

10. Make time for WE the COUPLE. Make romantic getaways a priority, especially when kids and job encroach! Schedule dates every week, especially when you have children. Go to marriage enrichment to learn, grow, have fun, get a tune-up, heal, and rescue your team.

11. Adhere to exclusivity as the key to a great sex life with your spouse. Channel your sexual interests, entertainment, and sensuality to that one person and one person only. Pornography, sexual entertainment, flirting with others, lustful imaginations about others all work to replace and douse the flame at home. The most satisfied marriages are those that have had the least number of partners, the least comparison, and the MOST loyal commitment. You invest by exclusivity: date more, plan evenings for sex, and ask each other about romantic and lovemaking preferences. Your sexual relationship is a place to please, to serve, to thrill your spouse—a place to invest, not to consume or even to coast.

12. Decide not to walk alone. Gather a support team around your marriage. Seek and socialize with couples and people who are *friends of your marriage*. You don't need supposed "friends" who tell you what they think you want to hear

while cutting down your spouse or undercutting your marriage. Ask a mature couple to mentor you, especially during a season of blitz.

13. Reach out to others. Help others. Connect with another couple, group, or class. Offer to help them. You can encourage, share your story, and invite them to go through a video-based marriage enrichment resource with you. Become a support system to them, and your investments will also help your marriage.[12]

10

Invest in Your Home Team

Each day of our lives we made deposits in the memory banks of our children.

Charles R. Swindoll

amily. The word can evoke memories, images, and feelings of our greatest happiness—and our deepest pain. Our most joyous triumphs and our most heart-wrenching blitzes. It's amazing and sobering how our major life events and perspectives can be determined by what happens at the foundational level of family.

Most areas of life demand a lot from us, yet I'd prefer not to use the word *demand* when it comes to family. Our marriage, our children, and our family don't demand much from us; they *expect* much! The problem is that the expectations are often unspoken and the tolerance level high. That's why we often get away with ignoring or shortchanging the desires and expectations of our spouse and our kids for a significant period of time. And when it all crashes down around us, we're surprised. We're blitzed.

The topic of family is a sensitive area. In fact, right now you may be thinking: *Jeff, don't go there.* We often feel that way because (a) whatever happens in our family reflects on us, and we want people to think well of us, and (b) challenges and failures in this area dredge up emotional pain.

Stay with me. Let's go there. When you're facing a blitz, you need to be able to lean on your home team, and they need to be able to lean on you too. Better together, remember?

Don't Compare

There's an ironic twist in perception when it comes to family, which causes us to look at others' lives through rose-colored lenses and our own through dirty ones. We compare other people's *outsides* to our *insides*. We know the heartache and stress and disagreements and challenges that we face inside the walls of our own homes and hearts, then label our own family by the worst-case scenario, by what's currently frustrating us the most. The last argument we had is the most recent assessment we have of ourselves.

On the other hand, we tend to look at other people and assess them according to what we see on the outside: their homes, their cars, their jobs, or their clothes. We see their kid has made the select softball or basketball team or has a 4.0 GPA. We see the faces and images they project in public, but not in private. We're not comparing apples to apples. We're comparing their best-shined apples to our moldy oranges. The truth is that no one can live your life but *you.*

So start with that—don't compare. Comparison comes from the consumer mind-set, a competitive, performance-based value system that, hopefully, we're learning to discard. This isn't to say we shouldn't be looking for good role models in others. We should. But it should be their humility, character, and quality relationships that attract us, not their external image and success. Be real. Respect authenticity.

181

I'm embarrassed to look back and think about the way I was envious of other couples over the years. One was another NFL quarterback and his wife. I viewed him as taller, stronger, more successful, and more popular. They appeared dashing, beautiful, and well-rewarded. He was an All-Pro, a popular Christian role model, and a fabulous speaker.

Looking back on it, my comparisons were a huge waste, even a drain on my being the most loving and honorable Jeff Kemp I could be. Too much attention went to looking at another person and family, keeping my attention away from appreciating the blessings I had and being my absolute best for the family with which I'd been blessed.

Years after I left football it happened in a different form. Stacy and I knew a couple in our former church. The impressions we formed from them usually made us think we weren't in their league when it came to spiritual maturity, marital unity, and family character shaping. They're quality people, but we found that their surface was better than their foundation. Sadly, they went through a divorce that came as a great shock to all who knew them. As is often the case in life, we didn't know them as well as we thought, and none of us knew of their challenges in time to effectively help them.

Don't waste time comparing your insides to others' outsides. It's much better to put your energies into investing in your family members and relationships.

Do We Pay More Attention to Work Performance Than Home?

I doubt there are many jobs that analyze and rate your performance as frequently or scrupulously as pro sports. The video doesn't lie, and the stats are constantly tabulated. Business has profits at stake, so they pay close attention to performance. At work, you'll hear about it if you don't watch your priorities and don't meet your team's expectations. You'll see what's happening with profits and losses. There are quarterly reports, along with an annual review, when you'll be held accountable for all these things.

In your family, the measurements are generally much softer. You can go a lot longer without feedback, therefore missing the signals saying you're not meeting the needs of the people around you. In your family, unfortunately, you can let bad things slide for too long if you're not paying attention.

There have been way too many times when I've been clueless as to how Stacy and I were really doing in our relationship. It usually becomes apparent after periods of busyness when I've been preoccupied, and then suddenly one night show great interest in my wife because I want a sexual connection. Only then do I find out that she's been wilting without relational connection. She'll say something like, "I really don't feel like we have a relationship right now." Whoa! I don't like to admit it, but she's right. That's when I realize I've let my focus on her slip. I've let *us* drop off my priority list.

We've all got to be intentional about keeping our priorities straight, expectations clear, and our needs and desires understood in the family. When I say "intentional," I don't just mean we need to have good intentions (you know what they say about those!). More than intentions, we need a plan.

I'm a huge visionary, but not so good on execution. My wife has endured more than a few birthdays or Mother's Days where I'd schemed for weeks about doing something really cool for her or buying her a special gift, only to get to the actual day and be scrambling to pick up some grocery-store flowers as I arrive home thirty minutes late for dinner.

Good performance requires a plan—a plan that actually gets executed. Say you're going on a business trip. You know what city you're traveling to and with whom you'll be meeting. You know what it is you want to accomplish. You plan it all out.

Say you're starting a business. You cast a vision and make a business plan to shape and accomplish that plan. Great football teams shape a vision such as, "We aim to be the dominant team in pro football and win numerous Super Bowls" (à la the late Bill Walsh).

But when you go into marriage and parenting, suddenly you're a *team* instead of an individual. The expectations of each of the partners begin to grow even if they're not voiced. The expectations and needs of the child(ren) are unleashed whether voiced or not, whether you anticipated them or not. You need a family plan as much as and more than you need a business plan!

Our family matters more than anything else. No influence in the lives of children is greater than the influence of their parents, who shape the home and family by the way they interact, their role-modeling of relationships, and their tone of either acceptance and love, or distraction and conflict. The family is what makes YOU happy or not happy. It's also the shaper of your child's happiness, character, and successful launch into life. With that in mind, why *wouldn't* we have a plan, a vision statement, a set of core values, and some basic intentionality for something as important as this?

The sad reality is that most of us don't shape a vision for our family the way we do for so many other ventures in life. I think of all the soccer and basketball teams I coached when our boys were little. We always had a team identity. We always had a vision for what we wanted to be and what we wanted to accomplish together. And we always identified core values to define us and help us get to where we wanted to go. Some of these included things like:

Respect
Encouragement
Hustle
Tenacity

Do you have values and principles that mark your family? If not, or if you've never written them down, let me strongly encourage you to engage everyone in your family and then develop yours.

Developing and Reinforcing Your Family's Core Values

Consider the rights of others before acting on your own feelings, and consider the feelings of others before acting on your own rights.

John Wooden

Here are some ways to reinforce your family's core values and demonstrate that they are your priority:

1. Pay attention to reentry on your way home from work.

As soon as you walk through the front door, dedicate your attention to your most valuable relationships. It's a good idea to find a landmark five minutes from home, where you can say to yourself, *I'm about to get home. I need to take all the work stuff that's filling my head and leave it right here.* Take a few minutes to calibrate what kind of evening or focus you want to have with your family. Concentrate on setting yourself up for a whole new environment, for their benefit and yours. Set aside the first five minutes at home to making your spouse, then your kids, feel noticed, appreciated, and affirmed. Sometimes I pray on my way home and ask God to help me have the energy and focus I need to love, and not shut down, when I get home.

2. Protect the family dinner hour.

Dr. Les Parrott, in *The Hour that Matters Most*, recommends a cooperative approach to dinner. With the busyness of families these days, don't neglect gathering together daily as a core family value. Make it a team thing. Do it *together*. Split up the duties when preparing different parts of the meal. Someone sets the table, someone handles the dirty dishes, someone thinks of dinner conversation questions. Make sure someone turns off the TV or puts on some background music. Every now and then do something memorable and special. Our family has a "special plate" we used on special days—birthdays, other celebrations, or simply when a child is feeling down and discouraged. You can have a distinctive place setting to set in front of a person on a special day to pour some love on him or her. Go around the table and have each family member say what's special about that person, speaking words of praise, encouragement, and affirmation. (Stacy had the special plate out for me the night I got cut from the Seahawks after a midseason game. "I love Daddy 'cause he's a good football player," said one son. The next one interrupted, "Be quiet. He just got cut." I guess humor counts too!)

Dads, Dr. Tony Evans points out that a man can lead, love, and shape his family with a regular, daily one-hour investment—the dinner table! Engage, ask questions, say a prayer. Discuss the news or the situations and challenges in your life and your kids' lives.

Praise and affirm your kids, and especially your wife. Assure them of your commitment and love for them. These are investments that will pay lifelong returns.

3. Show interest in what interests your kids.

Show interest in your children's homework, sports, art, computer program, or music. More important, show interest in the things *they* like. It may not be what *you* like, but it nourishes a child's soul to know you care. You don't go or watch or praise because it's the most impressive performance you've ever seen; what's important is what it means to *them* that you care, that you're there, and that you're invested in them. There's huge value in that.

I'll throw out a couple of warnings on this point. One is that it's very challenging in a conditional, performance-based society not to focus dominantly on the performance rather than on the person—the effort they invest and the character traits you see in them. Let your attention and encouragement be about unconditional love and character affirmation, not mostly performance-measured praise.

Also, don't own your children's experiences. Don't be maniacal in your enthusiastic embrace of what interests your kids. When you do that, you risk taking the ownership of the activity from the child and making it yours. I've seen that happen and it's ugly. It's totally inappropriate and leads to all kinds of dysfunctional behavior. (Think hyper Little League parent or the ridiculous "reality" show *Toddlers and Tiaras*.) So many talented kids have quit sports or music because of excessively intense parents. We raise and steward our kids. We don't own or exploit them. Let them have their own lives.

Focus on character, not just the performance, and that goes for the kids and for the parents. Parents weren't intended to wrap themselves or their kids around the sports schedule! Balance matters. Show interest, not rabid sports involvement or interference.

4. If you're married, date your spouse.

This can be a huge contributor not only to your marriage, but to the security of your children if they see you spending time with your spouse. Many parents think it creates more security in children to focus on the children first, but actually the opposite is true. When Mom and Dad make regular and special efforts to spend time together, they're making investments in themselves and their kids. When kids see that Mom and Dad love each other, children relax emotionally and feel more secure. Researchers have documented that ensuring the stability of their marriage is the best thing parents can do for their kids.

5. Express physical and verbal affection.

I was in a restaurant once and saw a dad tousling his son's hair and putting his hand on his daughter's shoulder. In fifteen minutes I saw hugs, little jabs, strokes of their hair, and many smiles. I was putting myself in their shoes and I felt great. And it made me miss being a dad when my boys were younger. Decide to make your love felt, heard, and seen. Use hugs, pats, texts, notes, and one-on-one experiences. How powerful it can be to simply take a child to breakfast or shopping.

187

As mentioned earlier, learn your kids' and spouse's love language. One of my sons' love languages is quality time. I'd often take him with me to the store, and he'd be my buddy. He loved it. One time I attempted to take his little brother along too. His response was to immediately hop out of the car because the dynamic had changed. All of a sudden it wasn't *his* time with Dad anymore!

Find excuses to spend one-on-one time with your kids. Establish rituals that are only "yours," like a special handshake, a little game, or sharing a milk shake. The greatest rituals could be putting them to bed, reading to them, or telling them stories from your heritage. There's no better time to tell a story than at bedtime. Oh, and keep up the hugs and kisses, fist bumps, and smiles through all the stages of life, all your years together. Public displays of affection may go out of vogue for a while in high school and college, but adapt, and don't quit. Affection is needed and is bonding nonetheless.

6. Catch them doing well! Praise and affirm regularly.

Do you praise the meals in your home, and the cook? Do you pull out the all-star list of awesome lawn-mowing efforts or meals made? Do you praise the dish-rinser and compliment the kid who set the table without being asked?

If you see a child refrain from retaliating against an annoying sibling, do you pull that patient child aside and affirm the character and strength you saw in him or her? Is someone the peacemaker in your family? Thank him and give him public credit if it doesn't embarrass him too much. Does someone in your family bring everyone laughter? Do you thank him or her for it? In any of these cases, make it a point to affirm these qualities in your family members and describe how appreciated and important they are to the family dynamic.

Look for the highlights, the little and big positives in your family. Thank them and praise them. Maybe even have a night where you make some funny awards that mix fun and honor to bring attention to great things in your home. Such affirmation breeds more of the good and contributes to the sense of family belonging and unity, of being a team.

Alan Shepard, one of the few people to ever walk (much less hit a golf ball) on the moon, was America's first astronaut in space. In an interview about the NASA space program, he gave an un-emotional analysis of his heroic experiences as an astronaut in the risky and heady days of our space program. The only time he got choked up was when he described a conversation with his dad. Alan's elderly father began by asking, "Al, do you remember the day you told me you were going to be an astronaut?"

"I sure do," replied Alan.

"Do you remember what I told you?" his father asked.

"Yes. You said it was a bad idea."

"Well, I was wrong."

At this point, the always-cool Shepard welled up with tears and said, "That's all he had to say."

Nothing mattered to this widely praised and admired American hero as much as the approval and validation of his father. Moms, dads, step-parents, are you making it a priority to validate your children?

7. *Pay attention to relationships.*

People who are primarily task-oriented like to get stuff done. Their inner tachometer is always running to accomplish things in life: pay the mortgage, save up for children's orthodontics, make sure there's money for the medical bills, keep a meticulously well-organized home, and accomplish their almighty to-do list. These are, indeed, important things. Ultimately, however, as revealed in objective research, our happiness is most directly related to *relationships*, the people with whom we share our lives. It's people who are others-centered, caring, generous, and loyal toward other people who rank highest in measures of human happiness, not necessarily the people who accomplish the most or keep all their ducks in a row.[1]

It's important for the person who's a gifted task accomplisher, with a doer/driver mentality, to look at the big picture. If this describes you, work with your personality. Write down some tangible goals related to how much time you spend with the family. Take meals together. Drop by the kids' bedroom at bedtime. Write notes to your child or spouse (love notes, not delegated memos!). The task of writing down the values and relational goals for your family might work well for all you doers/drivers, as well as for those who are more laid back.

8. Laugh and play together.

A lot of parents worry about their kids drifting away from them and not adopting their values. Honestly, one of the keys to addressing this is quite simple: Play with your kids and make your family fun! Horse around, take excursions, play sports. Laugh and play games together. That should continue all the way into your kids' college years and beyond. It's the sugar that makes the medicine go down. It's where memories are made. Fun, laughter, and play are among the ways children learn to bond and feel attached to their family. They create a fondness and appreciation for the family unit for everyone. And it helps children respect the values and beliefs the parents want to pass on to their kids.

For the most part, children are going to do what we *do* more than what we *say*. If your family is fun, it will make it less likely that your children rebel from the values you've tried to instill in them. It also creates more opportunities and fertile soil for teaching those values. When they know you care and they have positive emotions around the experiences they've had in your family, it increases the eventual stickiness of your beliefs and values.

9. Discipline, boundaries, and consequences.

It's true that too many rules without relationship equals rebellion. But it's equally true that children feel less secure and protected when their mom and dad fail to model authority for them. Kids need training in respect, obedience, and responsibility. They need to learn from our example and teaching to respect authorities, imperfect as they often are. They need us to be their parents, first and foremost. Some people have reacted so negatively to punishment that they threw out discipline. They forgot that the best discipline is not punishment, but training and consequences of facing reality. We need to set consequences that fit situations and allow natural consequences.

In our parenting team, my wife is better at letting our kids face natural consequences than I am. I'm so thankful she always saw we shouldn't be rescuing our kids from consequences, and that we shouldn't be afraid to let them dislike us, or our boundaries, for a while. Love includes discipline, and discipline is made up of training, limits, and consequences.

Keep Your Family's Love Tank Full

There's a stark difference between where a car can go when there's gas in the tank versus when the tank's empty. People have tanks too—love tanks—that need to be filled in order to operate well. Our children especially need us to fill their love tanks.

Our strongest-willed and wildest boy when he was little was Kolby. For various reasons he would more than occasionally throw tantrums and cause some serious commotion in the family. I remember my frustration with him one particular time when I was trying to think of some appropriate discipline (like a time-out in a soundproof padded room!). I was getting more and more intense trying to correct and calm him. Stacy recalibrated me. She pulled me aside and said, "Jeff, his love tank is empty. You've been gone a lot. He needs time with you. How about you take him outside, play ball with him, and spend some time with him?" What I wanted to do was draw the line, sit him down, and firmly discipline him. But I listened to my wife and, sure enough, as soon as I spent some time with him, his behavior totally turned around.

So often in the heat of pressurized family schedules and annoying behaviors we fail to see the patterns that bring out the best and worst in our children and ourselves. We think like a consumer, wanting to have a child give us the behavior we want. It makes so much more sense to think like an investor. An investor parent is going to realize that a child's behavior is often directly related to how secure he or she is feeling. To fill a child's love tank with time, attention, hugs, and affirmations is to give that child more of the fuel needed to be his or her best self.

At the same time, it's important to remember that training, boundaries, and discipline are complementary investments of love that parents make in their children. There are scores of children who are catered to or are allowed to get away with anything, but ultimately the parents lack the sort of love that trains a child and draws boundaries. A parent must be a parent. Expressing lots of affection and enjoying time with your child is the soil that makes discipline and tough-love boundaries take root.

Facing Family Problems

Investors look to the long term and don't expect immediate returns. They think creatively about the best way to ensure valuable outcomes. Here's an investor-minded parenting idea that may sound unlike anything you've ever heard, but if your teenage son or daughter has been slacking off or screwing up, consider it carefully: Turn your critical, examining eye on yourself for a bit. Consider what deep need, human respect, or common courtesies you may have been failing to deliver into his or her life. Look for ways *you* can be the one to apologize—for not loving well enough, for not spending enough time with the teenager, perhaps for not plugging into her life or giving her the honesty, respect, or priority she deserves. Try it. See what happens to your son's or daughter's conscience when you give him or her unconditional love and respect rather than a barrage of corrections and condemnation, or lectures about "getting with the program."

Maybe it's time to get real and tell your children part of your life story, including the feelings, insecurities, dreams, frustrations, and mistakes you experienced when you were their age. It may be powerful to share your screw-ups and lessons, as well as why you care so much about them and the great future they can have.

Blitzes happen in our kids' lives. Misbehavior, stupid stuff, rebellion. Life's blitzes, big or little, in children and teens present a crucial time for parents to ask themselves, "How much of my child's behavior is due to what he or she might be either copying from me or missing from me?" Lessons about life and making good decisions become a whole lot easier when a child's love tank is full. We can't expect a kid to operate well on an empty tank, any more than we can expect to drive a car without regularly filling it with gas. A child's love tank needs to be filled with love in its various forms—time, affection, affirmation, acceptance, encouragement, praise, and respect.

And because love does what is best for another, at a price to oneself, love must also include training, boundaries, and discipline. Ignoring these may be the very area in which some of us parents have failed to love our children. To humble ourselves, apologize for imperfect parenting, and share the tough news that boundaries and consequences will be firmed up may be the most loving thing we can do. Josh McDowell's phrase "Rules without relationship equals rebellion" has always stuck with me. The goal of parenting should be to always show affection and prioritize relationship in every season, using firm boundaries when children are young, and then loosening up over the teen years as they demonstrate and are given more and more responsibility.

The Assurance and Security of Love

Two of my sons have played college football under Coach Mike Swider, one of the winningest Division III coaches in America. Much more important, Mike Swider lives his life to passionately shape young men into men who serve others, men of character and courage who live for a cause greater than themselves. I love having that man pushing, loving, and shaping my sons. Mike is a committed father and begins each of his many public speeches describing why he is who he is. The reason is love—the rock-solid assurance of love, delivered to him by his now-deceased dad. In a speech titled "Living With No Regrets," Coach Swider painted a picture of what every child deserves from his or her dad (and mom, of course). Swider addresses men directly to confront the bigger deficit in society and encourages servant leadership in men:

> I stand before people as a product of something, the product of a father . . . something we don't see often enough these days . . . my dad.
>
> My dad was part of the Greatest Generation. He grew up a Chicago city kid with nothing and fought as if he'd had everything. At eighteen he was in the South Seas fighting in World War II. He comes back, gets an education, and spends the rest of his life teaching and coaching in the public schools of Chicago.
>
> It was never about him; it was always about a cause, about the guy next to him . . . about serving.
>
> My dad never made more than thirty thousand dollars a year in his forty-year career as a public school teacher in Chicago. Our culture doesn't value him. Yet the numbers of people who sent letters about his influence and who came to his funeral were off the charts. Our culture is missing those kind of guys . . . It was not about him. It was about others, a cause, about service.
>
> I had a father who affirmed three things in my life. I am a product of my dad. My father emphasized these three things every day. Every single night before I went to bed he would tell me these three things.
>
> First of all, "God loves you, son. The maker of this world created you with a purpose. You can do nothing to lose His love. You are not just something out there. He loves you. He's going to be faithful to you. He has a plan for you. Don't ever forget it." He told me that every night.
>
> Also, "I love you, son. I will always love you. You can do nothing to lose my love. No matter what happens, no matter how much I

challenge or confront you, I love you, and every action I take toward you is based out of my love for you. Don't ever forget that."

The third thing he told me is, "I love your mother. And I will always love your mother. Nothing will ever keep me from loving your mother." He proved it.

I was three for three, wasn't I? Most kids today are zero for three. Dads aren't telling them God loves them. Dads aren't telling them they love them, if they're even involved. And Dads aren't telling their sons and daughters they love their mother and will never stop that commitment to love her.

This is the way to build assurance and security and peace in a child. Most kids struggle. They need the assurance and security of these three loves. And you wonder why we have problems and issues in our culture. I'm not a rocket scientist, okay? I'm just a long-haired football coach.

We're trying to legislate and do all sorts of things to make our culture a certain way. But we missed the boat. God says this is the way we live: God loves you. Your dad loves you. Your dad loves your mom. I don't care how archaic it sounds; it's the truth, and the truth works . . . because the author of life is the one who decided the truth.

I want to encourage and challenge all the fathers, especially, and all the moms: That's your most important job.

Coach Swider simplifies it. Demonstrate and tell your kids daily that they are loved—by God, by you, and, if you're married, by your determined commitment to your spouse and family.

Right Priorities = Happiness

Over the last fifteen years, psychologists and social scientists have focused deeply on establishing an empirically based understanding about human flourishing, aka happiness. *The research is clear: People are poor predictors of what brings them happiness.*

One of the surprises out of this research is that money has very little impact on happiness. The richest Americans tend to be only slightly happier than the average person in the country. Another surprise is that generally people are happier at work than they are sitting on a beach in the Caribbean.

The initial reason for the push to spend more on the research surrounding happiness was to figure out why depression, anxiety, and other mental illnesses have been on the rise since WWII. The results suggest that people have become less and less aligned with living in ways that naturally produce more reliable levels of well-being and happiness, despite rises in material wealth and comfort.

> Many persons have a wrong idea of what constitutes true happiness. It is not attained through self-gratification but through fidelity to a worthy purpose.
>
> Helen Keller

For example, studies have found that many people have come to believe that happiness is defined as increasing one's frequency and duration of pleasurable activity. Self-gratification has become not only an accepted way of living, it's being prescribed as the way to achieve happiness from almost every media venue.

However, research found that personal pleasure only produces happiness if it comes as a reward to such behaviors as contributing, giving, gratitude, service to others, engagement in work, and living with goals tied to a purpose greater than one's self. When personal pleasure is the primary goal, happiness becomes less attainable.

Developed countries have pursued an idea of happiness that is, ironically, leading us further from the goal. We find instead that the most important component for achieving happiness comes with achieving a sense of connection with others. People are social by nature. They experience more happiness when they're with other people, when they prioritize the role of people and relationships in their lives and work.

Want to be happier? Goals and activities to serve others and develop closer, more considerate, and more satisfying relationships are the likeliest path to producing happiness.

Life is more than transactions. This is most true in our families, but also true in our jobs, businesses, and communities. People with a track record of overcoming blitzes and lifting others around them are the ones who recognize this universal truth and prioritize their lives accordingly.

At the end of the day, and the end of your life, it's your closest relationships that count. Are you investing in yours today? What do you want to do differently? Decide and do it.

Living Your Values

You can't run a business like this! That was my initial thought when I picked up my car, and my mechanic, Dave, told me there was no charge. "What? No way," I protested. "You just did seventy-five dollars' worth of work and spent some of that on synthetic oil and a new headlight. You've got to let me pay you."

He countered, "It's all good. I can occasionally do this if I want. You're a great customer who brings me all three of your family's cars."

Thinking of his wife and kids—and his business in this tough economy—I begged him to let me pay. He finally relented and said I could pay if I'd like, but not until the next time I came in. You can be sure I didn't switch to any other mechanic. I absolutely came back and have been recommending this relational and generous mechanic to others.

Dave lives with generosity—with grace, peace, and well-ordered priorities. He aims to serve and make others' days go well. He loves to give them kind surprises and breaks of generosity. Those are the values that bust the consumer mind-set and set people up for wins in their relationships AND in their workplaces.

Dave later told me his trade secret for surprising people with "no charge." He buys headlights in bulk at a huge discount. He could make a sizable profit on the margin, yet he prefers to surprise people by going the extra mile and giving value away. Whether the economic scales balance out or not, Dave enjoys his days, has positive interactions with people, sends them away happy, and carries a lot of that satisfaction himself.

This story illustrates what it can look like to live your values. A value is a belief system, a guiding principle, or a philosophy that determines your decisions, actions, and behaviors. These internal principles motivate you and demonstrate what's important to you. Your values are like a compass, pointing you in a consistent direction. Living your life (and making your decisions) without identifying and being true to your values makes you like a ship without a compass or a rudder. You wouldn't know where you were going or have anything to guide you there if you did!

Time Out for Self-Reflection

What would you consider to be your family's core values? Grab your laptop or a pencil and start writing what you'd like them to be. If you're married, ask your spouse to do this exercise too, and then talk about it afterward. Feel free to get your children involved too.

Following is a great values assessment from *What I Wish I Knew at 18* by Dennis Trittin.[2] Run it by your own family, adding values you've come up with that aren't listed here. Then circle the ones *most* important to you. Have each family member do the same, then discuss. Which ones are more important to which family members, and why? Narrow the list down and create your family's core values. Be creative with kids to design it together.

Personal Values

Healthy living	Spirituality/God-consciousness	Self-discipline
Fitness	Punctuality	Integrity
Commitment	Trustworthiness	Obedience
Courage	Purity	Humility
Honesty	Cleanliness	Sense of fun
Thankfulness	Loyalty	Industriousness
Financial responsibility	Modesty	Reliability

Social Values

Compassion	Justice	Kindness
Forgiveness	Grace	Flexibility
Hospitality	Gentleness	Righteousness
Faith	Patience	Generosity
Gratitude	Courage	Perseverance
Unconditional love	Contentment	Respect

Run the Play: Practical Application

- On separate occasions and in private conversations, ask each person in your family: What are some things I do that encourage, please, and help you? What are the things I do that discourage or frustrate you? What do you wish I'd do or stop doing?

- Turn a family meal into a "Special Person Occasion." In our family, we put a special plate at one person's table spot and then allow each person around the table to describe a trait or two they admire and love in the person being honored. Remember the story I told earlier about the night I got cut from the Seahawks? I remember that night for more than the laugh I got from my son. When it was Stacy's turn, she told my boys (and me), "I love your daddy because he loves God and has integrity." A rough time in my career was transformed as joyous tears filled our eyes that night. The love in our family was overcoming the blitz and indignity of being cut from my football team mid-season.

- Choose to serve others together as a family. Perhaps you could offer to clean up and trim an elderly person's yard, serve at a soup kitchen, or volunteer for shelters, nonprofits, or your church.

- Swim against the current and anchor your family with as many dinners together as possible (some families may need to make it breakfast, but dinners can last longer).

- To gain time for your family, and rediscover games and creativity, unplug your TVs for a week (and set your iPads and phones aside for a few hours). After a week, consider no TV for a month, or redefine and take back control of media in your home.
- Write little notes of love, affirmation, praise, and humor (only the kind that will be appreciated and enjoyed). Decide on a number of hugs and kisses you'll deliver this week to jump-start your affection for your spouse and children.
- Commit to telling your children of your love for them, and also God's love for them. In a divorce situation or blended home, assure them of your goodwill toward their birth parent, and your committed love for your spouse.

11

Leave a Lasting Legacy

*I don't want to be remembered for football or for
politics. My legacy is my family.*

Jack Kemp

My father left me a legacy that still pulses through my life. It's a
legacy of leadership, love, and lift. Naturally Dad was human,
flawed in his own ways. He had some childhood insecurities
that didn't really heal, some ego that blinded him a bit, failures
he couldn't make peace with for many years. I share those realities
in total love and respect for him, but I also share them to encourage you. You and I aren't immune from being influenced by our
struggles and regrets. Still, it's within your reach to impact lives,
to be remembered well, to leave a legacy.

I want to share with you more about who my dad was, the
impact he had on me, and the legacy he shaped. I believe there
are significant lessons we can learn from his life—his attitude,
his approach, his actions, and his words. The main lesson is that
who *you* are and the way you live—the way you face and overcome
blitzes—can be an incredible blessing in the lives of others.

Dad was born in 1935, the third of four sons to Paul and Francis Kemp, in Los Angeles, California. They were a competitive group of boys, and Dad's older brother, Tom, often outshined him in areas that mattered most to my dad—in sports like baseball, and especially in football, which was his obsession.

Dad channeled his insecurities and dogged competitiveness into football, persevering through the smallest level of college football (at Occidental College) and barely squeaking into the NFL in the seventeenth, and last, round of the NFL draft. He was traded once and cut twice before he finally landed a steady quarterbacking job in the new American Football League with the San Diego Chargers. In the greatest move of his life, he married my mom, Joanne Main, who also went to Occidental and was with him for twelve of his thirteen years, and five of his six teams, in pro football.

Dad's determination and perseverance propelled him, even when he was heartbroken by the Chargers. He'd finally become a star quarterback, but broke a finger on his passing hand. The Chargers tried to foil the league's rules to get an extra player on their roster, though the risk failed. And during the twenty-four-hour period allowing other teams to claim a player, Dad was claimed by another team. The Chargers were obligated to sell Dad for one hundred dollars to the Buffalo Bills. That blitz looked pretty negative, until his Californian wife, my mom, encouraged him to settle our family in Buffalo, where he quarterbacked the team to two AFL championships—ironically over those very same Chargers!

As Dad grew older, his passion for ideas and economics equaled his earlier passion for football. He was known for his love of books. He read histories, biographies, and especially books on economics. He read with a purpose. He wanted to know the way the world worked and how to make it better. He'd skip the card games on team flights or nights out with the guys in order to read these thick books! After leaving the NFL, he began an eighteen-year congressional career, representing the blue-collar voters of suburban Buffalo. He was a jock who made himself an intellect, a conservative who had run a labor union (AFL Players Association), and a white man who hung out with blacks as they faced down injustice during the civil rights era. He was the son of a motorcycle deliveryman, who bought a truck and moved from being an employee to employer. Dad passionately championed free enterprise and liberty for everyone, both in America and around the globe. He appealed to people of all backgrounds, ethnicities, and political parties, but not by targeting their differences. People respected or loved him because he honored their dreams and the American Dream that unites our amazing American melting pot.

Dad revered the Declaration of Independence and the God-inspired brilliance and courage penned in that document. He felt it was written for men and women of all places and all times. His heroes were Abraham Lincoln, Winston Churchill, Martin Luther King Jr., and Ronald Reagan. He voraciously studied economics, because he felt the right ideas and policies could free people and nations to thrive and grow to reach their potential. From Adam Smith to classical economists to Art Laffer's napkin drawings, Dad crafted his core belief that people and businesses respond to incentive-based low tax rates. He ran for the Republican nomination for president in 1988 and lost, but approached it as a happy warrior, thrilled at the chance to advance the American idea of liberty, free enterprise, incentive-based economic policy, and the opportunity for families to achieve bigger dreams for their children.

In politics, his focus was the people he served. Politics and government, he believed, were not about the person leading but about the people being represented: their dreams, their potential, their families, and their enterprising pursuits. His style of politics was not a campaign for candidates or personalities, but a campaign for ideas, principles, and policies. He believed in serving your party best by serving your nation first, in debating your opponent by presenting better ideas and policies, not by attacking that person's reputation or motives. His philosophy was that of the better thesis, beating bad ideas with better ideas, always offering a transcending solution rather than just opposing a position or policy. He was collegial because he was committed to ideas, not to winning or to defeating another party. He felt it was better to convert opponents than to beat them. Dad believed that people want solutions, not critics or showmanship. And solutions, he felt, occur closest to the people, in their own zip code, respecting the smallest building blocks of society: a family, a farm, a small business, a community of faith.

My dad spent four years as a radical reformer and champion of inner city empowerment and home ownership as Secretary of Housing and Urban Development. He loved that job because he got to focus on his forte: LIFT—creating opportunities and elevating examples of responsibility, resilience, and initiative among people fighting to lift their children and neighborhoods out of the discouraging bogs of poverty and government dependence.

Throughout his life, Jack Kemp believed that sports (especially football!) were a microcosm of our society and our competitive, team-oriented way of life. Our culture's spirit of healthy competition leading to productivity requires cooperation, where both the weak and the strong succeed.

According to Dad's view, people are lifted up not only by their own efforts, but by the inspiration and help they receive from those who achieve greatly. He championed the power of ideas, particularly "the American Idea," saying,

> The Declaration of Independence applies to every individual; everyone should have the same opportunity to rise as high as their talents and efforts can carry them. And while people move ahead, we should endeavor to leave no one behind.

As a pro football player, Dad lived through the era of the civil rights movement. By way of protest, he and his teammates walked out of restaurants, movie theaters, and hotels that refused to welcome black players. He learned and passed on the lesson that, just as in the huddle, everyone is equal. A great team is comprised of players with differing gifts and backgrounds, committed to each other around the same cause.

Bill Bennett described Dad as having "a sunny disposition, an optimism about people and situations." He strove to inspire and elevate others to be their best. He passed along a legacy of optimism, perseverance, teamwork, leadership, empowerment, and encouragement. He saw and fought for the dignity and potential of all people in all situations. He taught us to bring something good out of bad situations—to face and overcome our blitzes, and to help others around us do the same.

> Keep a clear eye toward life's end. Do not forget your purpose and destiny as God's creature. What you are in his sight is what you are and nothing more. Remember that when you leave this earth, you can take nothing that you have received . . . but only what you have given; a full heart enriched by honest service, love, sacrifice, and courage.
>
> Francis of Assisi

When a Life Becomes a Legacy

When I was asked as a kid what I wanted to be when I grew up, I was quite literal when I answered, "A pro quarterback." That's what my dad did, and I loved playing football in my backyard, so that's what I wanted to be. Growing up with a father who was a football star and a significant national political leader naturally creates an environment of achievement and status expectation in a firstborn child's life. Sometimes it's a ray of sunshine; other times it can be a cloud of excessive expectation—either of others, or in my case, my own.

I believe my parents did a noble job of raising us kids with as much unconditional love as they could and as little performance pressure as possible. Thankfully, my dad was a huge force for good in my life. I'd never have persevered through twenty years of Little League, high school, college, and professional football without my dad's constant voice of optimism and patient confidence:

"You're in your right place."

"Your day will come."

"Think like a starter. It's only a matter of time."

Those words echoed in my heart and still do today. Dad gave me a vision of the world, a vision of the greatness of America because of the faith and universal ideas upon which it was founded, a vision of inspiring and lifting other people's vision of themselves. He imparted to me a vision of championing the underdog and seeking the lost sheep. When we left the home, he told us kids, "Remember, you're a Kemp; be a leader." He gave me that vision of my role as a leader and a vision of God's ultimate and good plans. I continue to meet people from all over the world who tell me of their respectful affection for him and how he inspired them. What a legacy! He had his quirks, human weaknesses, and flaws, but he was a powerful force in many lives besides mine. Dad was strong, indefatigable (I had to use that favorite word of his!)— so seemingly larger-than-life that I never even contemplated his mortality.

In late 2008, I experienced a weird and deep blitz. Dad was having problems with his hip, which he thought was football-related. He was feeling under the weather more often than we'd ever remembered.

I was at a leadership retreat for nonprofit leaders in my field of marriage and family strengthening. One morning I was sitting next to my friend from Seattle, Marvin Charles. Marvin grew up without a father, running the illegal side of city streets. Today he runs a prolific mentoring program called Divine Alternatives for Dads Services (DADS), for fatherless men and disconnected fathers who want to become good dads. As a song was being sung, a thought hit me for the first time ever: *Dad may really be sick someday. He will die eventually, and it could be much sooner than I've ever imagined. Wow. What will that be like to lose his presence in my life? How much will that affect me?*

Within seconds I was welling up with tears. My heart was racing, and Marvin could tell something abnormal was happening to me. Marvin is a huge, strong, humble, and tender man. He

206

reached over, put his heavy hand on my shoulder, and asked me, "Brother, are you okay?"

I said, "I think I'm gonna cry, Marvin." The floodgates of my heart's emotions opened up and I sobbed for ten minutes. Marvin's presence and hand on my shoulder gave me a freedom and an assurance that fully facing my newly realized fear and the depths of my love for my dad were okay. In fact, they were good. Marvin prayed for me, and I spent the last two days of the retreat in an altered state of somber realization and sadness. I was grieving the eventual loss of my father.

I have to believe that God was preparing me. Within a week, a doctor's X ray revealed that Dad's sore hip wasn't an old football injury. His hip and much of his body was compromised with metastasized cancer.

Realizing Dad was mortal, and anticipating the last chapter of his life could take him from us much sooner than I'd thought possible, was the deepest blitz I'd ever faced. The diagnosis of stage-four melanoma and the suffering he went through certainly became a large part of that blitz for all of our family. But my most intense emotional blitz had come the week before—even before we found out that Dad had cancer. It was almost as if God allowed me to go into a very dark emotional place, just so I could grieve before the actual chapter of his illness and death would come.

Very soon I was asking God, "What good can come from this?" I wasn't angry with Him. I wasn't trying to change His mind. My thought was, *This is where we are; this is the reality we have. No sense hiding from it. Let's engage and see what God has for us.*

Could I spend this time with Dad? Could I find a deeper level of relationship with him through this? Could we experience a deeper level of dialogue and needed conversations we'd not had before? How could I be an encouragement to him? What did I want to say to him and hear from him before he departed this life?

Truly our family came together during this blitz. Our relationships became slower-paced, our conversations less issue-based and accomplishment-oriented. We got down to the essentials of "I love you . . . you love me. I appreciate you . . . you appreciate me. God is good . . . this is hard . . . but we have His love and presence with us."

We took the approach of facing the blitz as we worked through this season. Dad knew his cancer was terminal and that he would die from it, but he chose to take the chemo and radiation treatments for his family's sake. He wanted to be a fighter for us, so he went through them. He took on his blitz with an others-centeredness without complaining.

My siblings all lived near Mom and Dad and stepped up to serve so well. My younger brother stepped up to tackle all the logistical matters. The unity and teamwork in the family were special.

I flew back to the East Coast from Seattle four times during those four months. On one flight I wrote a letter listing all the things for which I wanted to thank Dad. I described the legacy he'd given me in my life. I asked Mom to sit with him as I read to them my three-page list of thank-yous. There was laughter and a lot of smiles, and of course tears. I wanted there to be hope that he would recover, but I knew realistically that was probably my last thorough tribute to my dad. It was joyful, painful, encouraging, sad, deserved . . . and awesome.

On my last visit I saw that the cancer had progressed significantly, and Dad's condition had deteriorated. I read him passages out of the Psalms and New Testament. I prayed for him as we both lay on his bed at home. Sometimes he'd pray, even though he hardly had the strength or the breath. Knowing I was about to return home, I asked him if he'd pray a prayer of blessing over me. I'm not sure he was thinking of a patriarchal prayer like the kind in the Bible or that Jewish fathers have prayed over their children for generations, but he wanted to do it. I'll never forget it. He told me he loved me and prayed, one more time, the legacy and leadership mantra I had gained from him and my mom all through the years. They were the last words he ever said to me, his last prayer.

"Heavenly Father, help Jeff remember his talent . . . the difference he can make . . . and help us both remember that the only thing that matters is 'Thy will be done.'"

As it turned out, the emotional grief I encountered before Dad's diagnosis was a gift. I had done my deepest grieving before those intense four months of Dad's treatments, cancer, and death. What could have been the worst of times turned out to be times of rich intimacy, amazing courage, and memorable affirmations of love and gratitude.

Besides the legacy that came from the way he lived his life and related to us, Dad left a legacy in writing, in various forms. He had written occasional letters and frequent notes to me all his life—"JFK-grams"—since those were his initials. He did the same to my siblings and his grandkids. (I'm repeating this practice with my own kids, and plan to continue with their children.) In those notes, he provided me with

1. Extravagant affirmation of my identity and talents.
2. Confident affirmation of the difference I can make in this world with my leadership.
3. A worldview that God is loving and good, that we can trust Him no matter what, and we yearn for His will because He knows all things better than we do.

Dad wanted to make sure I knew what he thought of me and how he believed in me. That prayer and all those notes are tangible reminders of his legacy and of his confidence in me to carry on lifting others, just as he did.

Expanding the Reach of a Legacy

My father both taught and modeled the principle of legacy to me from my earliest years. He wanted me to learn from him, to be sure, but he also wanted me to learn this principle from others. We were committed to family dinners, and many times Dad would bring home leaders from Congress and have them converse with me and my siblings.

One evening it was U.N. Ambassador Jeane Kirkpatrick and her husband as they were enjoying my mom's macaroni and cheese in our dining room. Dad prodded the ambassador, "Jeane, explain *détente* to Jeff." It wasn't just dinner conversation. It was really a dad equipping his children for confidence and engagement in the adult world, the world of ideas. He was communicating to me, *You WILL be a leader. You need to understand the world. You WILL have a significant place in it through how you serve and the legacy you leave.*

Of course, my own kids have rolled their eyes at me when I get too intense and ask dinner guests to explain things to my boys. But it's all part of the bigger picture, of building a life that's capable of and committed to investing in the people around us, and making a contribution in this world. Life is about being an investor, not merely a consumer. That philosophy is part of the legacy I received from my parents. It's the legacy we should all want to impart to our children, and the legacy we hope they will leave behind them as well.

Passing It On

When my son Kolby was fifteen, the two of us boarded a flight to Detroit. We were headed to see the Seattle Seahawks play in their first ever Super Bowl. It was a pretty exciting father-son adventure. In the row in front of us we saw two big guys, brothers, in their twenties, completely decked out in Seahawks jerseys and gear. They were in a jovial mood, clearly exuberant to see their Seahawks play in the biggest of games. I remarked about their enthusiasm, and they gushed about the Seahawks and how their dad had taken them to every single home game since they were little boys. I didn't tell them I'd played for the Seahawks a decade earlier, but was getting a kick out of the passion these guys had for the Seahawks, and especially for their dad. They told Kolby and me that after all the games to which he'd taken them, they were thrilled to be taking him to the Super Bowl with them.

"We have him up there!"

I was a little perplexed about where their dad was, until they pointed out that he was—*ahem*—in an urn, up above us in the overhead compartment. Or rather, his ashes were. Fifteen-year-old Kolby figured it out a bit more slowly, then crinkled his face, looked at me, and said, "Dad, that's weird!"

The jovial brothers went on to tell us that the reason they were so fanatical about football was because of their father. He'd raised the brothers taking them to the Seahawks' summer training camp, watching games together all season long. It was something they did, and loved, together. That was his legacy to his sons. And they were honoring his memory by taking him, in the best manner they could, to the Big Game.

I don't know if I share that story more for levity or inspiration, or just because I love it. Maybe all three! But my point is this: You're going to leave a legacy in some manner—how will *you* be remembered?

Someday each of us will have a tombstone laid over our physical bodies (unless we're scattered in the ocean or taken to the Super Bowl in an overhead compartment) with a chiseled remembrance to our life, two dates with a dash in between. What will that dash mean? What will you be remembered for in that dash? How do you *want* to be remembered?

Great accomplishments?

Impressive titles?

The accumulation of wealth?

A lifestyle of self-indulgence?

For your achieving power and exerting control?

Or would you most want to be remembered for having given your best to people, for having loved and lifted others? That would be a legacy of love and LIFT.

Living to Prosper Others

Central to facing blitzes and leaving a legacy is the discipline to take the long-term view, our first strategy. Keep the end in mind, not just the present moment. This brings us to the idea of transition, or *succession*, especially when it comes to organizational leadership. The same principles are as true professionally as they are personally. Though the dynamics may be different in a business scenario than in a family, the overarching questions remain the same:

How will you be remembered?

What kind of legacy will you leave behind you?

How are you preparing the next generation of leaders to carry on well after you're gone?

One of the hardest things for organizational leaders to see—especially founders and entrepreneurs—is the importance of transition planning. All too often, the focus is on *What can I build for now?* instead of *What can I build for later?* When we focus on living for the benefit of others, we think about those who follow us. We build an example, a reputation, a legacy. It causes us to love, to train, and to empower others. Just like with raising children, we need to transition by equipping, launching, and then letting go.

Riches, fame, and personal success are transient, whereas a legacy *endures*. And it not only endures, it passes on to the next generation, and the next, and the next. . . .

How to Pass the Baton

It's crucial in transitioning leadership, just as in a relay, to pass off the baton so that the person running the leg after you can grab it. What is his/her position in relationship to yours? How can you make the most efficient hand-off possible so the whole team wins?

212

How can you make it easier for the next person to run his or her leg of the relay?

It takes a lot of maturity to understand that you need to empower and spur on the people coming next to *go past you*. What you say as a leader still carries a lot of weight, and people are looking to you for guidance. You need to honor and encourage the new leaders. For example, if you're an outgoing leader, put yourself in the shoes of the new incoming leader. You wouldn't want your predecessor to be voicing opinions and speeches that compete with your authority, would you? Instead, you must demonstrate your confidence in your successors, especially in the presence of those they'll be leading.

When I was playing for the 49ers, Joe Montana was always as helpful as he could be when I was the starter in his absence due to injury. He quickly moved from acting like the starter to the role of backup. Remember, the backup has to support the starter. He watches him and helps him. He keeps an eye on the field and interprets the defense to assist the QB who's playing. For Joe to so quickly move from one perspective to the other—for my benefit and the team's—showed humility, maturity, and team spirit. But I wasn't replacing Joe permanently. That's what is so impressive about QBs like Trent Dilfer and Matt Hasselbeck, who were fiercely competitive but shifted their focus to supporting and lifting the quarterbacks who replaced them.

That's the mind-set I'm talking about, the attitude that can build and leave an enduring legacy—whether in a family, a business, a ministry, or a community. It's about being willing to switch from starter to backup (or vice versa), sometimes at a moment's notice, and always being ready to do so.

Leaving an Organizational Legacy

The professional football world and the business world can be intensely dog-eat-dog, and many times transitions are brutally abrupt. It often takes a while for a new system to be assimilated, for the ropes to be learned, and new people to start operating well. But when established people are helpful mentors—teaching the ropes, systems, and culture—*the whole transition goes a lot more smoothly.*

I was the founder and president of Stronger Families and ran the organization for eighteen years. Many wonderful donors and board members and staff helped us to build a solid legacy of supporting families in the Northwest. I was always ambitious for us to do more, grow more, and improve our initiatives and impact.

We eventually reached a point where I was no longer the best person to lead and manage the organization into the future. My talents were not taking us further as an organization, and running an organization probably wasn't the best platform to focus on my strengths and leadership opportunities. And it was time for the organization to reinvent itself and grow in new ways. But it took a blitz (as it often does) to help me make a change.

In late 2009, we fell far short of our fund-raising and contract revenue projections and ended up in a debt position that was not tenable, threatening our very future. We'd just come through the year-end period of highest donations and were out of funds, owing money to staff, landlords, and vendors. The blitz required that we come together with our board and face reality.

I remember well the pressure and desperate nature of things. Often in the mornings, I wouldn't want to get out of the shower to face the situation. I was hoping and praying for some solution I couldn't yet see. It was discouraging and hard, but together we faced it directly.

I'd always taken a positive interest in our communications director, Noel Meador, a very talented and committed young man. But I hadn't officially prepared or tutored him for transition-type leadership. Fortunately, I had hired a fabulous former business executive and military general, Jimmy Collins, to be our CEO. He had been mentoring Noel in leadership. That legacy-creating foresight became essential when, along with my CEO and board,

I decided the best way to save the organization and carry on the mission was for Jimmy and me to resign and subtract our salaries from the equation.

We made significant downsizing decisions, but the best decision we made was to hand off the organization and its leadership to Noel. He took the executive director role, and we volunteered our time to fund-raise and help downsize until Noel could right the ship. He did, and all of us are thrilled that a great organization is alive today, as thousands of families are being helped because of Noel's leadership and vision. A deep financial blitz forced my wife and me to consider that what we'd built with the organization was complete, and it was time to open our eyes to a new and yet uncertain chapter in our life together. We faced reality; we came together with our board and our leaders. We grasped a bigger vision and new options. We lifted a new, young leader. Sacrifices opened the door to a revived organization and a new national role for me with FamilyLife, my present employer. I'm grateful for everyone's role and sacrifice in facing this blitz. But, ultimately, credit and thanks go to God for all that was learned and experienced through that intense season of facing a blitz. Trusting and turning to Him was the source of my hope, peace, and power.

Perhaps you're finding yourself in a blitz like mine, or realizing that someday you're going to leave your current position, and leave well. Here are some ways to ensure you leave a lasting and honorable organizational legacy:

1. Force yourself to think about the future, when you'll no longer be in the picture.
2. Become a mentor and pass on your values, culture, and wisdom to the next generation of leaders. One-on-one lunches and informal gatherings with younger leaders are perfect for this!
3. Involve your whole team in determining and shaping a distinct culture of core values that matter to you and to them.

4. Delegate more and more. Drive decisions down to leaders in training.

5. Begin transition planning. Engage people in determining how the organization will be led in the future. Create a plan for that process.

We'd do well to learn in business what is more apparent, but still not easy, in parenting: Our goal is to work ourselves out of our roles and launch our children into flight. So with that in mind, let's look at leaving a legacy in our families.

Building and Leaving a Family Legacy

When my then-twelve-year-old son Kyle's Sunday school teacher asked for volunteers to answer a question, his hand shot right up. The lesson that day was about using words and speech to build people up, not tear them down.

"What do you love to do, Kyle?"

"Play football."

"Great. Imagine that you're playing a game, but it's not going well. People are criticizing you, making fun of you, calling you names and saying all sorts of negative things. Imagine if everyone there was booing you, Kyle. How would that make you feel?"

Kyle immediately piped up, "Like my dad."

I laughed like crazy when I heard about this exchange in his class. I was glad to have another affirmation of my son's sense of humor, but I'll admit to being a bit less crazy about being the object of that humor! Ouch . . . he must have been to that game when I got booed and benched.

The only real negative to this story is my own vanity. I'll be remembered for more than being booed. The positive is that, in the bigger picture, my kids know the real me and are quite comfortable with that person. They know we can laugh at ourselves in our family (and have reason to!). They know their dad's not perfect, but that I persevere despite the odds, opposition, and criticism. They know that I love them, their mom, and God. And that's a good legacy to leave.

What's true in football and business is also true for families. We want to be remembered for what counts. And we want to pass on a legacy of empowerment to the next generation of leaders coming up behind us.

The bottom line is, we want to be remembered in such a way that they smile, respect us, and live out our values. That's success. *That's legacy.*

Now, you may be thinking, *That's easier said than done.* Clearly. But that's the way it is with all good things. Nonetheless, we can pass on a legacy if we're intentional, consistent, and persevering. And, friend, the good news is this: If your heart is sincere and good, that's going to transfer to your children. Take heart in a truth from football—second halves are full of great comebacks. How you finish matters more than how you started. It may take some courageous doses of humility and apology, followed by sincere efforts to make the future better from this day forward. Here are some ideas I've learned—from my parents, my wife, and others along the way—about how to instill a legacy in your own family:

1. **Make sure you fill your children's love tank.** As mentioned earlier, do they get enough of your time, attention, and affection on a regular basis? And do they know that God loves them even more than their parents?

2. **Give them a sense of great value and significance.** Affirm that they count. Let them know they're special: cherished, honored, and respected. Make them a priority in your day. Remember my dad's JFK-grams. How are you communicating affirmation to your kids?

3. **Help strengthen their sense of calling to serve others and impact the world around them.** Instill more than belief that they're beautiful or accomplished (which are not components of their character), and focus on what they have

to offer others (e.g., "You have a beautiful spirit of caring and encouragement," or "Your courage makes you a great influence and leader with people," or "You have a way of bringing hope to others who are going through hard circumstances.").

4. **Give them a compass, not instructions.** An excess of instructions (being overly controlling) disempowers our children and takes away their initiative and sense of creative responsibility for their own lives. If you give them a map with only one route highlighted and all options blacked out, they're likely either to reject it or fail to develop their own navigation skills. A "compass," on the other hand, is a set of core beliefs and practical virtues, including the ability to think through long-term consequences. These things are beneficial to relationships, setting goals, facing blitzes, and being a resilient person. At some point you have to switch from giving your kids rules to giving them principles. That's the difference between a map and a compass.

5. **Be honest and transparent.** Admit your errors. Apologize when you offend them. Be real. These are crucial if they're to truly receive what matters. Give them a deeply embedded sense of what is right, what is wrong, and what is *best*. They need that in order to carry on after you're not around. To be transparent with your children means you trust them, which grows their trustworthiness.

6. **Give them a sense of context, allegiance, and genealogy.** I remember hearing quotes from my dad for years that we "stand on the shoulders of giants." Because we live in America, we are free. We can reach for our dreams. Nearly all of us have computers; we've got roofs over our heads; we're wealthier than most people in history. We owe so much to grandparents and parents, those who sacrificed for us, giants like the soldiers who have defended our freedom, the statesmen who advanced the cause of liberty, the teachers who inspired us,

and the entrepreneurs who created the software to power to-day's companies. We need to teach our kids to see themselves in the tapestry of ancestors, leaders, organizations, servants, and family members who have gone before us. Gratitude is the posture of humility, and humility is the start of great things.

Imparting a Blessing

The concept of speaking and praying blessings over the next gen-eration has largely been forgotten. It used to be more common. But traditional cultures still believe in and practice it regularly. The Jewish patriarchs, for example, understood the power of blessing. Their traditional writings tell us that Abraham blessed Isaac, Isaac blessed Jacob, and Jacob blessed his twelve sons.[1] These blessings were not just rote recitations or positive wishes. If you read through the Old Testament accounts of these people, you'll discover that the blessings they prayed actually came to pass!

What does a blessing look like? This was shown in *Fiddler on the Roof*, the 1971 film adaptation of the 1964 Broadway musical of the same name. In one of the most touching musical scenes from the movie, the father, Tevye, blesses his daughters prior to the Friday night Shabbat meal, as has been done for thousands of years at Jewish tables. The song, called "Sabbath Prayer," gives a wonderful model for blessing our children, calling for them to be strong, to be good mothers, and to always love the Lord. He sings,

> May the Lord protect and defend you.
> May He always shield you from shame. . . .
> May God bless you and grant you long lives.
> May the Lord fulfill our Sabbath prayer for you.[2]

A blessing is an unforgettable legacy each of us can leave to our children or anyone else, for that matter. Anyone can do this, if done with authenticity and sincerity. When communicating a blessing, you will want to include

1. Affirmation: *You are a unique and valuable person who is deeply loved.*
2. Encouragement: *You have a bright, meaningful future ahead of you.*
3. Favor: *Doors will open for you when you walk in your calling with faith, integrity, and perseverance.*
4. Hope: *You will overcome, you will accomplish, you will see your dreams come to pass, and you will make a difference in this world.*

When you impart a blessing, make eye contact and place your hands on the person's shoulders or head. The spoken word is very powerful. There's a proverb that says, "Death and life are in the power of the tongue."[3] You can use the power of blessing to leave a legacy of affirmation, encouragement, favor, and hope in the lives of the people you influence.

They Must Increase While We Must Decrease

There's an account in the Bible of the "hand-off" from John the Baptist, whose mission was to point to the coming Messiah, to Jesus. It was time for Jesus to start His earthly mission and for John's influence to wane. Rather than try to hang on to his followers and maintain his fan base, John humbly deferred to Jesus, saying, "He must increase, but I must decrease."[4]

There's a lesson in this for all of us. This is what every mom or dad should (eventually) say of a child. This is what an athlete should say of the teammate who takes his/her position. This is what a leader should say of the next person who takes the reins of the organization or ministry.

The words of God himself toward Jesus tell the rest of the story: "This is my Son, whom I love; with him I am well pleased."[5] Those words mean so much yet are heard by so few people. And the lack of those words is what puts people into a lifelong pursuit of trying to find love and affirmation, many times in all the wrong places. I can tell you that many pro athletes are maniacally driven to succeed in an effort to gain the elusive admiration and approval of their fathers. Giving a blessing is intentionality of affirmation, of respect, of unconditional love, and is a vision for a positive future.

What would it mean if your children heard this from you?

Your grandchildren?

Your employees?

Those who are taking the baton of leadership from you and running the next leg of the race?

I encountered this very situation when I was handing over the reins of leadership of Stronger Families to my successor. Stronger Families was my baby. I had helped birth it and raise it and was passionately committed during its formative and most turbulent years. Could I now take my attention away from what I wanted and how I wanted to be remembered, and step back so that Noel could increase and I would decrease? Could I stand back and be an available mentor but not a dominating force? Could I allow a new, younger leader to shape the organization in his own way?

With the helpful reminder of a blitz, I did. And he has. (I credit God, His grace, and answers to desperate prayers.) And it has been a win-win for us individually and for the organization. As I stepped back, I had no clear vision for how my future would unfold, but I had a sense of what was best for Noel and for Stronger Families. What may appear to be bad can turn for good when we focus on teamwork and lifting others above ourselves. Noel has improved the focus and depth of the organization in ways I could not have done, with different gifts and a unique vision.

What Is Your Legacy?

Abraham Lincoln left a legacy. Dr. Martin Luther King Jr. left a legacy. Mother Teresa left a legacy. Parents and grandparents leave a legacy. You can leave a good legacy. And if we're parents, there's no greater legacy than our children.

A loving, resilient, and growing marriage can also be a great legacy, a true inspiration to others who will follow. A legacy can be the mark you make by caring for and inspiring the children you teach, the youth you coach, the people you mentor, the employees you build up, or the organization you shape.

> Children are the living messages we send to a time we will not see.
>
> Neil Postman

A legacy begins with being humble enough to see yourself for who you are and reality as it really is. Decide today who matters to you, those who will travel after you. Build into those relationships. Make sure your priorities, your schedule, your checkbook, your actions, and your words are aimed at a cause greater than your own advancement or pleasure. Your legacy can start today. Perhaps it's an apology and a reconciliation that may begin the shaping of that good legacy.

What will be your legacy?

Time Out for Self-Reflection

1. Think of someone in your life who has influenced you in a significant way. What was it about this person that touched or shaped you? What words would you use to describe him or her?

2. If your children, co-workers, or employees were asked what kind of legacy you'd left in their lives, what would you want them to say about you?

Run the Play: Practical Application

1. If you're a **parent**, identify some tangible goals for what kind of legacy you want to leave your children (apart from financial security and other material goals). Think about

things such as character, faith, their worldview, steward-ship, appreciation of art, literature or music, social justice, compassion, and service. In each virtue and goal, identify something specific you can habitually do to make sure the message is being communicated.

2. If you're an **organizational leader**, identify tangible goals for what kind of legacy you want to leave your employees (or clients, company, organization, community). Think about things such as integrity, kindness, creativity, respect, gener-osity, and impact in the community or the world. In each category you choose, identify something specific you can ha-bitually do to make sure the message is being communicated.

3. Write a letter to honor, thank, and bless your parents, or any other special persons who invested in you. If you can, deliver it and speak the words directly to them.

4. Write letters to your children or grandchildren. Value them, validate them, affirm them, encourage them. Declare your favor and God's favor and hope for their future. Plan an ex-perience they would enjoy to give them the letter and speak your blessing to them.[6]

Conclusion:

Find Your Power Source

Light of the world, shine on me
Love is the answer.

Todd Rundgren

I can do all things through Him who strengthens me.

Philippians 4:13 NASB

Life is about relationships. Relationships are the essence of family, of teamwork, and of a cohesive society. A meaningful life is about love, because it takes love to make relationships work. But for that to happen, we need a power greater than our own, a source deeper than our own reservoir.

Facing life's blitzes is ultimately an opportunity to find and practice a deeper love. Sudden loss, unexpected disappointment, and vicious opposition all create pain and suffering. However, they also offer a summons to look for more than comfort and success. If the perspective is large enough and the horizon far enough, what we find is a summons to unconditional love—both to accept it and then to practice it.

In October 1992, I faced a blitz that athletes hate to face: the unwelcome end of my career. A month earlier I had been the last player released from the Philadelphia Eagles' roster, as they failed to make a trade for me to join another team before the season began. As I boarded the six-hour flight home to Seattle, I felt deflated and lonely. I remember the confusing contrast of grief over being rejected in football with a longing to reunite with Stacy and my boys. Coaches and other friends in the NFL reminded me of my value as a highly experienced backup QB. They told me that within weeks one of the NFL teams would likely face a quarterback injury situation and would call to sign me.

The weeks passed. I was feeling overlooked, not too hopeful, and was praying for a team to call me. Then in the fourth game of the season, my friend and former Seahawk teammate Dave Krieg got injured. My hometown team needed an experienced QB. I could envision the answer to my prayer: I'd go back to the Seahawks, my family would stay in our home, we wouldn't have to move to Philadelphia, and the kids would stay in their school. I'd finish my career as a Seahawk. It would fix my circumstances and fulfill my dreams.

I called the new head coach, Tom Flores. He had roomed with my father on the Buffalo Bills years earlier. We were family friends, and he'd been the Seahawks' general manager during the prior years when I'd played on the team. I left Coach Flores a message that I was in town, in shape, and hoping to join the team and offer my help. Within a day I got a message back on my answering machine. "Sorry, Jeff. We're going another direction and will be signing a QB from the World League. Good luck." *CLICK!*

My gut dropped. I went out the front door of our home and sat down on the porch. I hung my head, muttering to myself. My feelings were raw, and my thoughts went something like this: *I can't believe it. This is brutal. It's not fair. It stinks. I've been praying to you, God, but I'm not gonna pray. I'm just gonna sit here and feel this stinking pain.* I began my own pity party, feeling about as dejected and flattened as I had ever felt in my life. I wasn't losing my spouse or a child. I hadn't received a diagnosis of cancer. I wasn't going to jail or losing my marriage. But I was losing my career—and a lot more of my identity than I'd expected to lose when I stopped being a football player. My attachment to my career was proving to be a larger part of me, and my attachment to God was proving to be smaller than I would have described. I was losing my career, and it was the most painful blitz I had faced to date in my admittedly quite fortunate and blessed life.

I sat there—feeling the pain, marinating in the frustration, magnifying the unfairness and indignity of it all. Then my closest teammate came into the picture. My strong, loving wife with her very different personality style and gifting stepped out onto the porch. Stacy has a deep faith in God. She's convinced that no matter what we see or face, God is both good and loving. This temporary world may be fractured and flawed, but God remains in control, and His mysteries will never obscure that He's good toward us. She came out to bring me tenderness and love. She wanted to encourage me.

> If you allow it, [suffering] can be the means by which God brings you His greatest blessings.
>
> Charles R. Swindoll

"Jeff, I can't imagine how much this hurts. But I do know that we've been through many tough chapters, and God has always revealed His good purpose and plan after we walked through them."

I wasn't in the mood to be consoled, so I quickly snapped at her, "I know that." My tone was angry and dismissive. "I just can't believe that my career's finishing like this. After all I've been through, I just want to finish with some *dignity*." I was nearly growling, crushed by the frustration and desire for a better finish to my career than I was getting.

Stacy's intent was to encourage me, to lift me to a better state of mind. But she saw it might take a little more of the tough-love approach. Her voice was still soft and consoling, though when she heard me grumble about dignity, she changed her tack.

"I don't recall Jesus leaving the earth with much. You know, as I recall, when Jesus completed His life on earth and departed, He didn't get any dignity." A brief pause. "Maybe you need to consider letting go of that desire."

My reply was terse: "Maybe you need to go inside!" (I wasn't practicing sound husband communication techniques!)

Stacy politely returned indoors, leaving me to my grouchy pity party. But as she exited the scene, her words entered my conscience in a powerful way. Looking back on it now, I was in one of my life's most intense and transformative places. My worst life moment was about to turn into one of my best. My hurt, angry, pitiful emotional cocktail was about to become as sweet as any moment in my life. My biggest blitz was about to turn into my greatest epiphany. Leaving pro sports is usually pretty tough for guys. Having your identity stripped in a day, and losing the camaraderie of the guys and the intense adrenaline of NFL competition is a real shock. The inflated adulation that goes with the game is quickly deflated, the competitive athletic purpose to your life suddenly gone.

But because of what Stacy said, an overwhelming mental vision started to form in my head. In a flash I was envisioning Jesus' perfect life, His honesty, His courage, His compassion, His love. A perfectly loyal, humble, and others-centered life. He was the only man ever with no sinful arrogance, no selfishness, no lust, greed, or hatred. After being cheered on Palm Sunday as He entered Jerusalem with throngs of people shouting "Hosanna!" and worshiping Him as Messiah and King, He faced a brutal turn of events: Less than a week later, He was sold out by a supposed friend, Judas.

More than ever in my life, I was imagining and feeling the emotion as He agonized and sweated drops of blood while praying for strength to endure His mission. He knew it would entail giving up His life. He was arrested, falsely accused, falsely tried, falsely condemned to die. He was abandoned by most all His disciples and followers. As I sat on the porch, trying not to pray and soak in my pity, the picture of Him crystallized for me. I envisioned His being beaten and whipped by Roman guards to within inches of His life, then trying to drag the heavy cross up the hill to the place of His crucifixion.

Since junior high school, I'd been clear in my belief that Jesus Christ is the Son of God, sent to the earth as a man to be God's predicted solution to the human dilemma. I believed in Him as my Savior and Lord, but even after many years of pursuing growth in my faith in Jesus, my view of the magnitude of God's love for me was still relatively miniscule. My emotional sense of loving and appreciating God for His love was a lot less tangible than what I felt for my wife or children. Yet in the middle of this career collapse and pain, I considered the indignity Jesus underwent in His sacrifice for humanity—His sacrifice for me.

Like a tide rising faster than expected, an emotional wave started to come over me. I was experiencing His love. I was deeply feeling my love for Him grow as I felt His love for me. Tears came to my eyes. My selfishness and ingratitude became clear to me. I started to see my football career as a gift God had given me, not as an earned right that I was unfairly losing. The cup I'd been seeing as half empty became way more than half full. It became an epic moment in my life, one in which I felt more of God's love for me than ever before. I became grateful for football—humbled rather than grumbled. Even more than that, I was grateful for God's love, for His sacrifice, for His forgiveness, for His blessings. My blitz, combined with Stacy's challenge, was making God's love palpable, transcendent . . . real! With her help, and God's presence, I was seeing the big picture, the long term, the whole story. I was changing and being made ready for the new career I faced. I was confronted with the futility and dysfunction of focusing on myself.

Three Lenses and Three Strategies

Can you see the three lenses for viewing life, and the three strategies for facing blitzes, coming into play in my blitz? Stacy and I have a team approach to our marriage and life. She is the crucial teammate I called upon. Her compassion and presence encouraged me. Her truthfulness and commitment to what is best for me led her to speak candidly about my obsession with seeking dignity at the end of my career. She helped take me out of a consumer mind-set about what I was losing . . . to that of an investor. I could use my football platform to serve others. When I was at the end of myself, the bottom of the emotional barrel, I looked up. Loss and pain were drawing me into God's loving presence, and I was being given His power to forget the past and move into the future. TEAM IDENTITY. INVESTOR MIND-SET. A GREATER POWER SOURCE. These three lenses make all the difference!

I stepped back to take a long-term view, to see the bigger picture. Instead of just looking at the moment, and my loss, I became grateful for the past and aware of the future. Soon I was envisioning the positive difference I could make in a new career focused on helping others. I opened myself to change when I became grateful for God's love and the football career He'd given me. I let an intimate experience of considering God's love melt, move, and humble me. The epiphany that emerged from my interrupted pity party canceled my myopia and revealed how much I was loved. As I look back I can see that I learned to embrace more humility, more gratitude, and the importance of not defining my identity as a football player. My blitz felt big, yet put in its proper context, my problems were small. It was time to reach out to encourage and help others.

TAKING A LONG-TERM VIEW. BEING WILLING TO CHANGE. REACHING OUT TO OTHERS BY LOOKING TO THE TEAM AROUND ME. The three strategies helped me to face my blitz!

My "I'm not praying to God" vow didn't last too long. Soon after immersing myself in consideration of the life, death, and resurrection of Jesus, I was sensing God's love as never before and was overcome with gratitude to Him. Thanking God and adoring Jesus became spontaneous. I couldn't *not* pray! I heard what seemed like clear words in my mind: *"Forget what is behind me and do my best to reach what is ahead.*"[1] I suddenly felt free to let go of football.

The blitz of my career's sudden and early end burst the bubble of my own little view of my life. It exposed my selfishness, expanded my horizon, and opened me up to God's transcending love. Love changed me when I opened myself to see and receive it.

Within months I decided to accept the leadership role of the small start-up nonprofit organization at which I would spend the next eighteen years. That mission to help families has continued and expanded in my current role at FamilyLife. Building vision and hope for marriages and families has been rewarding in profound ways—ways that football could never provide.

Looking Upward Instead of Inward

I am the vine; you are the branches. If you remain in me and I in you, you will bear much fruit; apart from me you can do nothing.

John 15:5

I know that, for my part, I cannot fix and free myself from my problems on my own. That's why I always try to look both inward *and* upward. To me, this means simply looking to my Creator and the comfort, guidance, and help God provides. Confronting a blitz can compel you to seek a deeper relationship with your Creator or grow in your journey of belief and faith.

"Is there actually a Creator?" you might be asking. Is there a unifying purpose and eternal hope for us? Does my body constitute my total self or am I more than flesh, blood, and bones? Do I have a soul—and if so, what shapes its destiny?

C. S. Lewis once said, "You don't have a soul. You are a soul. You have a body." This is the perfect expression of what it means to take a vertical view of the world, our circumstances, and ourselves. A vertical view includes God and the realm of our faith: the eternal and spiritual.

Blitzes challenge and test your faith. Have you lost touch with the power of your faith? Have you ever really known, or perhaps forgotten, how to pray and ask for God's help? Maybe you feel like a victim. Where will you get the power to dig deeper than you ever have before?

My friend Joni Eareckson Tada sustained a horrendous blitz at the age of seventeen when a dive into the Chesapeake Bay left her a quadriplegic. Her blitz has been one that lasts a lifetime, yet she's drawn on God's power in her weakness to reach out to others and has had a tremendous impact on thousands and thousands of people over the last several decades.

Joni says, "The Bible goes to great lengths to remind us how weak we are, and how strong God is. God allows hardships to remind us of our desperate need of Him. Jesus said, 'Blessed are the poor in spirit.' In other words, 'Blessed are you when you come to me in empty-handed spiritual poverty.' It's the ability to recognize our weaknesses—and to boast in them—because then, and only then, can Christ's power rest on us. God always seems bigger to those who need Him most."[2]

Don't let your self-reflection stop with you and your relationships. A life blitz gives you the opportunity to explore the deeper issues of your soul: What is my purpose in life? Where am I going? Where is my faith placed? What kind of relationship do I have with God? Why am I broken, and how can I be forgiven and healed? Will my quest for success satisfy, or is there something deeper that will?

A blitz gives you an opportunity to be self-reflective about these things—to reconnect to the original, the eternal, and the ultimate—to things like forgiveness, reconciliation, and grace. It's the discovery of truth, hope, and love. The greatest discovery is that these things are not merely concepts; they are a person. That person is real to me. He is Jesus. He is God—and He changes lives.

Great teams hug each other after big wins and championships. And when asked, "How'd you do it?" they often respond, "We loved each other." In other words: We sacrificed to help each other do our united best. That's the sports version of love. *Ubuntu*. I am . . . because we are.

Facing life's blitzes calls for teamwork of the highest order. It calls for friends, for help, for camaraderie. It calls for being humble enough to be transparent and ask for help. It calls for shifting from a sole focus on self to a focus on caring for and helping others, even when we're deeply hurting.

Facing the disappointments of an imperfect world, with flawed people and natural tragedies, makes us look for more. If it makes us look for relationship with God, and to care for others, we're on our way to experiencing and giving love. From there, relationships gain hope. The discouraged gain encouragement. The beleaguered gain support. That's why *love* is the answer, and the only perfect source of love is God. Please consider that it wasn't God who left us, but we who left Him. We want to be in charge, to do things our way, to find glory and satisfaction in things God created, not in Him, the Creator. It's me who has messed up this world. We all have. But there's great news. Like the prodigal son discovered, the Father will welcome a humble child back no matter what he or she has done. There is no pit too deep. There is no mess too large. There is no sin that He will not forgive. You cannot stray too far from God's grace. He will welcome the humble child with lavish love and an eternal home.

Viewed through the perspective of the blitz, Jesus Christ faced and transcended the greatest blitz in history. The arrest, crucifixion, and burial of Jesus appeared to be the worst thing that could ever happen to a man, much less a perfect man. Yet within three days, His resurrection and appearance to five hundred witnesses and followers achieved the ultimate triumph that defeated death once and for all. Jesus looked to the long-term joy that awaited Him in the future. He humbled himself in order to offer himself as a supreme sacrifice for all of us who could never heal our rebellious break from a perfect God.

God's solution for humanity's rebellious break from their Creator came in the form of a converted blitz. Bad became good.

The short term was reversed in the long term. God was willing to humble himself to be born in a stable and later to die as a man. In the greatest act of selflessness, Jesus turned to bless others. God the Father, Son, and Holy Spirit collaborated, like a team, to bring reconciliation to the world. Jesus was and is the ultimate relationship investor. The limitless power of God's love turned tribulation to triumph.

Trouble, loss, and tribulation are not one-dimensional. God put himself through the worst of human experience—rejection, suffering, and death itself. The outcome was transformative and glorious. This is a model for us. It is a power for us. It's *the hope* for us.

May your blitzes be turned to good as you turn to a loving, all-powerful God, a caring team, and an investor identity. These will fuel you as you proactively take the long-term view, open yourself to be changed, and aim to be a blessing to other people. May your life be a great source of LIFT in the lives of others, even as you are blessed by those who lift you!

Notes

Chapter 1: Find the Opportunity in the Crisis

1. Unabridged Merriam-Webster, "blitz."
2. Many thanks to Leslie Mayne, founder of the Permission to Start Dreaming Foundation, www.raceforasoldier.org.

Chapter 3: Embrace a Bigger Vision

1. Honorary degree recipient Conan O'Brien's commencement address to Dartmouth College graduates, 2011, http://www.dartmouth.edu/~commence /news/speeches/2011/obrien-speech.html.

Chapter 4: Take a Deep, Honest Look at Yourself

1. Matthew 7:3

Chapter 5: Cultivate a Relational Value System

1. "Two Brothers" is based on a Jewish fable—a Talmudic legend, if you will. Other contemporary versions of the story include "Brotherly Love," in *Angels, Prophets, Rabbis and Kings*, from *The Stories of the Jewish People* by José Patterson (New York: Peter Bedrick Books, 1991); *The Two Brothers: A Legend of Jerusalem*, retold and illustrated by Neil Waldman (New York: Atheneum Books for Young Readers, 1997); and "Two Brothers," retold by Elisa Davy Pearmain in *Once Upon a Time: Storytelling to Teach Character and Prevent Bullying*, (Greensboro, NC: Character Development Group, 2006).
2. Email exchange with Dr. Gary J. Oliver, MDiv, ThM, PhD, executive director of the Center for Relationship Enrichment and professor of phychology and practical theology at John Brown University, Nov. 5, 2014.

3. Jim Collins, *Good to Great* (New York: HarperCollins, 2001).

4. Ken Blanchard and Mark Miller, *The Secret* (San Francisco: Berrett-Koehler Publishers, 2004).

5. Patrick Lencioni, *The Five Dysfunctions of a Team* (San Francisco: Jossey-Bass, 2002).

6. Proverbs 8:17; Jeremiah 33:3 and 29:13

Chapter 6: Be an Investor, Not a Consumer

1. *Media Matters*, "Our Rising Ad Dosage: It's Not as Oppressive as Some Think," February 15, 2007, https://www.mediadynamicsinc.com/UserFiles/File/MM_Archives/Media%20Matters%2021507.pdf.

2. "The Benefits of Gratitude," accessed online November 26, 2012, http://www.psychologytoday.com/basics/gratitude.

3. Dennis Trittin, *What I Wish I Knew at 18: Life Lessons for the Road Ahead* (Gig Harbor, WA: LifeSmart Publishing, 2010), 30.

Chapter 7: Look to the Team Around You

1. Genesis 2:18

2. Lencioni, *The Five Dysfunctions of a Team.*

3. Matthew 20:28

4. Marcus Buckingham and Curt Coffman, *First, Break All the Rules: What the World's Greatest Managers Do Differently* (New York: Simon & Schuster, 1999).

5. Arbinger Institute, *Leadership and Self-Deception: Getting Out of the Box* (Berrett-Koehler Publishers, 2000).

Chapter 8: Leverage the Power of LIFT

1. Patrick Lencioni, *Getting Naked: A Business Fable* (San Francisco: Jossey-Bass, 2010).

2. 1 John 4:19

Chapter 9: Strengthen Your Marriage

1. Genesis 1

2. Genesis 2:18

3. I work for FamilyLife, a donor-supported marriage and family training Christian ministry. For help and to help others, visit www.familylife.com.

4. The study of men and women, ages 15 to 44, was done by the National Center for Health Statistics, using data from the National Survey of Family Growth, 2002.

5. I want to thank my friend, esteemed marriage therapist, author, and strategist Bill Doherty who first developed the concept of consumer marriage. He developed his consumer marriage quiz in his highly valuable 2001 book, *Take Back Your Marriage*. His helpful websites are drbilldoherty.org and dohertyrelationshipinstitute.com.

6. Communication researcher Dr. Deborah Tannen and relationship guru Dr. John Gottman rate these as the fundamental relational needs of humans, with

the majority of women emphasizing their predominant need for love, and men emphasizing their need for respect. See Dr. Emerson Eggerichs's transformative teaching at www.loveandrespect.com.

7. Dr. Gary J. Oliver, Nov. 5, 2014.

8. Gottman Private Couples' Retreats, "The Scientific Basis for The Orcas Island Couples' Retreat," 2009, http://www.gottmancouplesretreats.com/about/relationships-research-conflict-friendship-meaning.aspx.

9. Friedrich Nietzsche, "Letter of August 1886."

10. I've picked up this idea from my friend Gary Smalley, the man who greatly helped Stacy and me, as well as millions of other couples.

11. John Gottman, PhD, *Why Marriages Succeed or Fail* (New York: Simon & Schuster, 1994).

12. There are many excellent resources to support and grow healthy marriages. FamilyLife, for example, has served over one million couples at the Weekend to Remember marriage getaways. For info, go to www.familylife.com and click on Find an Event. If you'd like a video resource to strengthen marriage relationships, consider *The Art of Marriage*, a six-week DVD series that Stacy and I use with groups. It is a practical and biblically based resource from FamilyLife. See theartofmarriage.com. For resources without a faith component, consider the National Healthy Marriage Resource Center at www.healthymarriageinfo.org.

Chapter 10: Invest in Your Home Team

1. Dr. David Mashburn, summarizing research results from *Authentic Happiness* by Martin Seligman (New York: Simon & Schuster, 2002); *Flourish* by Martin Seligman (New York: Simon & Schuster, 2011); *Flow* by Mihaly Csikszentmihalyi (New York: Harper and Row, 1990); *Flourishing: Positive Psychology and the Life Well-Lived*, eds. Corey Keyes and Jonathan Haidt (Washington, DC: American Psychological Association, 2003).

2. Trittin, *What I Wish I Knew at 18 Student Guide: Life Lessons for the Road Ahead*, 24–25.

Chapter 11: Leave a Lasting Legacy

1. Genesis 25, 27, and 48–49

2. "Sabbath Prayer," from *Fiddler on the Roof*, music by Jerry Bock, lyrics by Sheldon Harnick.

3. Proverbs 18:21 NASB

4. John 3:30 NASB

5. Matthew 3:17

6. To explore this deeply, read *The Blessing: Giving the Gift of Love and Acceptance* by Dr. John Trent and Dr. Gary Smalley (Thomas Nelson, 2011).

Conclusion: Find Your Power Source

1. Philippians 3:13 GNT

2. Email communication with Joni Eareckson Tada, July 16, 2013.

Jeff Kemp grew up in an atmosphere of professional sports, politics, and national leadership. He majored in economics at Dartmouth College and earned his MBA with honors from Pepperdine University School of Business. After quarterbacking at Dartmouth, his career in the NFL spanned eleven years, playing for the Rams, 49ers, Seahawks, and Eagles. Most years he played as a dependable backup quarterback. His best seasons came in 1984 when he led the Rams to the playoffs, and in 1986 when he replaced the injured Joe Montana for nearly half the season, helping the 49ers make it to the playoffs. Jeff and his father, Jack (former HUD secretary and VP candidate), were the first of six NFL father-son players. Jeff's underdog status and sharing of the personal rejections he faced in football serve to build a bridge to the experiences of others.

Jeff has invested his off-season time and private pursuits to charities, Christian ministries, and speaking to student, youth, and business groups. He chose a career in nonprofit service and team-building leadership to improve the lives of children by strengthening fatherhood, marriages, and families. In 1993, Jeff founded Stronger Families, serving as the organization's president for the next eighteen years, during which he and his team networked with leaders from all segments of society: business, community, church, military, government, and the media. His work at Stronger Families helped to unite many communities around strengthening marriages, and today Stronger Families assists military couples in protecting their marriages.

Jeff has been active in the marriage-and family-movement for over a decade. His articles have appeared in *USA Today*, *FoxNews Online*, the *Seattle Times*, and *American Enterprise*.

As a popular speaker, Jeff has keynoted for many events, from corporate conferences, association meetings, Governor's and Community Prayer Breakfasts, to youth and athletic events. His radio program, "Family Matters," was carried by sixty radio stations.

In 2012, Jeff joined Dennis Rainey and team as vice-president and catalyst for helping others at FamilyLife, speaking at men's events, marriage conferences, and occasionally on FamilyLife's daily show. His networks include the Marriage CoMission and Fatherhood CoMission, National Coalition of Ministries to Men, Pro Athletes Outreach, Athletes in Action, Fellowship of Christian Athletes, NFL Players Association, NFL Alumni, and The Jack Kemp Foundation.

Jeff has coached various youth sports for nearly twenty years. He and his wife, Stacy, have been married for over thirty years and enjoy mentoring young couples. They have four sons and two daughters-in-law. To learn more, visit JeffKempTeam.com or FamilyLife.com.